Teacher Certification Exam

Educational Media Specialist Library

Written By:

Marilyn C. Rinear, MS. Education
BA English

To Order Additional Copies:
Xam, Inc.
99 Central St.
Worcester, MA 01605
Toll Free   1-800-301-4647
Phone: 1-508 363 0633
Email: winwin1111@aol.com
Web   www.xamonline.com
EFax   1-501-325-0185
Fax: 1-508-363-0634

You will find:
- Content Review in prose format
- Bibliography
- Sample Test

XAM, INC.
Building Better Teachers

"And, while there's no reason yet to panic, I think it's only prudent that we make preperations to panic."

PRAXIS: Educational Media Specialist Library
ISBN: 1-58197-022-6
9781581970227

PREFACE

Any library media candidate, familiar with the State of Florida, Department of Education, *Study Guide for the Florida Teachers Examination: Educational Media Specialist PK-12*, will immediately notice that the competencies and performance indicators in this guide do not follow the state's numbering sequence. As I began to organize my thoughts and resources, I determined that a hierarchical approach from discussion of laws, standards, principles, and issues to specific operational concerns was more suited to my organizational style. Therefore, at the end of each performance indicator discussion, the state's competency/skill number will be indicated; i.e. my 4.1.7 is DOE 9.5.

Also I chose not to indicate resource cross references in my Table of Competencies and Performance Indicators. Instead they are cited by number opposite the DOE competency/skill numbers in the text itself.

I have not deleted any competencies though I have grouped some skills into single performance indicators for the sake of brevity. I added the section on the school library media specialist's role as a technologist. I hoped to produce a guide that is efficient without being cumbersome. In an attempt to avoid redundancy, I have used parenthetical cross-references to other indicators within this text.

My resource list follows MLA style with which this author is most comfortable.

INTRODUCTION

The increase in instructional technology has been accompanied by a need for an increase in library media specialties. The school library media specialist in the 1990's has been forced to assume responsibilities in an ever-expanding job description. When *Information Power* appeared in 1988, AASL-AECT recommended national guidelines for school library media programs. That definitive document recognized the teaching, information giving, and instructional consulting roles, listing eleven major functions of these roles and dozens of specific activities to perform. Since 1988, the explosion in emerging technologies has added the roles of technology instructor, technology (design and use) specialist, and media technician.

When the Florida DOE was revising the FCTE Table of Competencies and Skills for school library media specialists, the original survey listed 25 competencies, divided into 124 skills which ultimately were consolidated into 27 competencies and 90 skills. Just one of these skills - keeping abreast of the new developments in information science - could be a full-time job.

Today's school library media specialist must face the reality of increased responsibility coupled with flagging budgets and decreased support staffs. Exciting challenges require stalwart individuals who can forge a destiny for their profession.

Research in the last twenty years has continually reinforced the correlation between good school library media programs and student achievement. Promoting the library media program and soliciting support from administrators, teachers, parents, and students becomes of prime concern. With backing from all vested groups, the media center will flourish.

Welcome to the career of school library media specialist. This study guide will provide information on the essential competencies for mastering the entrance exam for this challenging field.

Marilyn C. Rinear

December 1996

Competencies/Skills   **Page Numbers**

Competencies/Skills	Page Numbers

COMPETENCY 1.0 UNDERSTANDING OF PROFESSIONAL DEVELOPMENT FACTORS.

SKILL 1.1 Update knowledge of state and national legislation and their impact on school library media programs.

National:

1965 Elementary and Secondary Education Act Title III

This legislation impacted school libraries by encouraging their expansion into media centers.

1981 Education Consolidation and Improvement Act

Chapter II of this bill included regulations and funding in the form of block grants for school library media resources and instructional equipment. Funding ended with the 1994-95 school year.

1995 Innovative Educational Programs Legislation

This three-year program provides block grants for innovative uses of technology in schools, including library media centers.

State:

1986 State of Florida created a special appropriation of 17 million dollars in matching funds for upgrading and expanding library media materials and equipment in public schools.

1990 State of Florida provided funding for SUNLINK, the DOE Division of School Library Media Services for retrospective conversion of public school libraries to create statewide interlibrary loan network (funding continued through 1996-97).

1991 Blueprint 2000, a System of School Improvement and Accountability.

This legislation transfers authority for the design of effective programs to local control and mandates formation of school improvement plans to hold schools accountable for performance of students.

Though library media programs are not specifically mentioned in the Blueprint 2000 goals, Goal 4 charges schools with the provision of a conducive learning environment, a goal enhanced by a successful library media program.

1993 Florida State Statutes address library media as follows:

231.15 specifies that like other certification areas - teacher, guidance counselor, principal, and athletic coach - a school library media specialist must meet the law requiring certification in her content area (1.7).

233.165 specifies that selection of instructional materials, library books, and other material used in the public schools shall meet the standards of materials propriety.
1. The age of the children who normally would be expected to have access to the materials.
2. The educational purpose to be served by the material.
3. The degree of mature classroom discussion of the material.
4. The consideration of the broad socioeconomic, ethnic, racial and cultural diversity of the children.

This article also prohibits the procurement of material with hard-core pornography.

233.34 dealing with funding for instructional materials, specifies that library and reference books may be purchased from the 50% of the instructional materials allocation that need not be ordered from the state adopted list.

DOE 22.1, 22.2   16, 18, 41

SKILL 1.2 Evidence knowledge of the concepts of AASL/AECT guidelines for library media programs.

National guidelines for school library media programs are provided in documents published by the American Association of School Librarians (AASL), a division of the American Library Association (ALA), and the Association for Educational Communications and Technology (AECT).

Information Power: Guidelines for School Library Media Programs, a collaboration of AASL/AECT, was published in 1988 to provide standardized national guidelines as a vision for school library media programs into the 21st century. The AASL/AECT Standards Writing Committee and contributors from public school districts and universities across the country, using standards that have been revised over the last thirty years, created a definitive work.

These revised standards reflect the flexibility to manage today's library media centers and to direct centers into the future. The AASL/AECT mission objectives are echoed in President Bush's message during a speech at the 1991 White House Conferene on Library and Information Services. The following is a summary of the guidelines culled from these and other publications.

1. A democratic society guarantees the right of its populace to be well-informed. To this end, libraries and media centers of all kinds are the bastions of intellectual freedom.

2. Literacy for all United States residents begins in the public school system. School readiness through access to ample media stimuli, facilities that provide physical access to materials across cultural and economic barriers, and a sound national goal, supported by legislative funding, will ensure that Americans can avail themselves of the information to which they are entitled.

3. Americans will become more productive in the workplace by taking advantage of the technology offered in the Information Age. To support the school-to-work initiative, school library media centers must offer access and instruction in emerging technologies used in business and industry.

4. Collaborative efforts between schools, business, and community agencies will encourage life-long learning. *Information Power's* mission statement and the vision statements of many public schools specify life-long learning as their primary objective. Thus libraries, even in the schools, must become community centers, offering their materials and services to all segments of the public. Such open access also motivates school-aged students as they see adults continually seeking information and educational opportunities.

[Specific guidelines addressing personnel, budgets, resources and equipment, facilities, and leadership are included in discussions of performance indicators throughout this guide.]

DOE 24.2   1

SKILL 1.3 Identify and examine sources which provide information pertaining to school library media programs.

In the list of resources at the end of this guide are many titles which provide information on school library media programs. *Information Power* (AASL/AECT), *Taxonomies of the School Library Media Program* (Loertscher), and *Administering the School Library Media Center* (Gillespie and Spirt) are three of the best-known and most accessible.

Less accessible but a valuable reference tool is the six volume set titled *School Library Media Annual* (Smith, Aaron, and Scales, Eds.), each volume dealing with different aspects of school library media programs.

The Florida DOE's *Florida School Library Media Programs: A Guide for Excellence*, though twenty years old, still provides sound guidelines for media programs. Many of the recommendations are only now being implemented in some schools.

Among periodicals *The School Library Media Quarterly* (AASL) offers scholarly articles that are research based. *The Florida Media Quarterly*, a publication of the Florida Association for Media in Education, offers many excellent articles written by Florida educators and each issue has a concise legislative review. *Media and Methods* presents information on integrating media into the curriculum. *Tech Trends* (AECT) examines the impact of technology and innovations in media use.

DOE 26.1   41,47

SKILL 1.4 Use research to improve school library media programs.

The task of administering programs in modern school library media centers can be daunting to the newcomer, whether the new graduate with a degree in information science or the experienced classroom teacher with 30 hours of library science. There is now so much outstanding resource material and the technology to easily identify these resources that the task can be managed by following a few simple steps.

1. Rely on the information provided in this guide's resource list. If your school or district's professional library does not contain these resources, visit the public library in the nearest large city or a university library where information sciences are taught.

2. Give your school media program a close examination before doing your research. Study any written evaluations by media personnel, school improvement committees, library advisory committees, or annual reports. Informally survey a cross-section of students and teachers to gather input about their perceptions of the materials and services that are provided.

3. Make a list of questions based on the concerns that result from your evaluation. Peruse the questions in Chapter One of *Information Power* to see if there are any pertinent areas that have not yet been addressed.

4. Do your research.

5. Produce a written evaluation of your school's library media program based on your findings. Submit this evaluation to the principal and plan with her the best way to communicate the information to students, teachers, and parents.

6. Gather input from all groups to whom your evaluation is presented.

7. Meet with the Library Media Advisory Committee or equivalent group to formulate program changes. Be sure to include students and parents or lay community members on this committee.

8. Implement the changes and plan subsequent evaluations.

DOE 26.2   47

SKILL 1.5 Share relevant research with instructional staff.

One of the fallacies of education is that all good teachers keep abreast of changes in education by reading professional journals. Many do and most try, but the volume of available material is overwhelming. Since the school library media center houses general professional materials and knowledge of the contents of these materials is one of the specialist's responsibilities, a vehicle for communicating information to teachers is important. A two-part NCR form that identifies the receiver, the resource title and date of publication, and a concise summary of the contents is easiest. Sometimes a photocopy of relevant portions of the article can be attached to the form. Save one part of each form for your own program evaluation.

Education Digest, Phi Delta Kappan, and *Educational Leadership* are outstanding trend evaluators. Such magazines as *Teacher* give information about grants and services for both students and educators. Each year FAME sponsors the Jim Harbin Student Media Festival. Students in four age groupings devise up to ten-minute programs in a variety of media. Winners productions are presented at the annual FAME conference. This is an excellent project for television production classes, but it is also a way to involve content classes in learning through media production. Look to the annual fall edition of the *Florida Media Quarterly* for complete details and application forms.

Of course, changes in school board policies, legislative actions, and DOE publications are usually channeled through the media specialists. The Florida DOE *Monday Report* is accessible through FIRN (the Florida Information Resources Network) and printed copies are sent to all school principals. Your principal may be delighted to have you offer to communicate information from that and other reports to teachers.

DOE NA

SKILL 1.6 Identify guidelines that define the library media specialist's role.

In addition to the AASL/AECT guidelines (1.7) also endorsed by the NEA, guidelines are available from state departments of education. *Florida School Library Media Programs: A Guide for Excellence* delineates areas of proficiency for all media center personnel. Developed as a result of the AASL/AECT's *Media Programs: District and School* (1975) recommendations, the Florida guidelines were prepared by a task force with almost 50% representation of active school media specialists whose input reflected the skills necessary in the schools in the 1970's as well as those that would be needed in future decades.

DOE 21.1   1, 15

SKILL 1.7 Identify the library media specialist's responsibilities from AASL/AECT guidelines.

The following summarizes AASL/AECT guidelines.

The role of the school library media specialist is three-fold.

The information specialist meets program needs by providing
1. Access to the facility and materials that is non-restrictive - economically, ethnically, or physically.
2. Communication to teachers, students, administrators and parents concerning new materials, services, or technologies.
3. Efficient retrieval and information sharing systems.

The teacher specialist is charged with the responsibilities of
1. Integrating information skills into the content curriculum.
2. Providing access to and instruction in the use of technology.
3. Planning jointly with classroom teachers the use and production of media appropriate to learner needs.
4. Using various instructional methods to provide staff development in policies, procedures, media production, and technology use.

The instructional consultant uses her expertise to
1. Participate in curriculum development and assessment.
2. Assist teachers in acquiring information skills which they can incorporate into classroom instruction.
3. Design a scope and sequence of teaching information skills.
4. Provide leadership in the use and assessment of information technologies.

DOE 21.2   1

SKILL 1.8 Identify professional organizations on local, state, and national levels.

Library Media Organizations

National:
1. American Association of School Library (AASL)
    American Library Association
    50 East Huron Street
    Chicago IL 60611
2. Association for Educational Communications and Technology (AECT)
    1126 Sixteenth Street, NW
    Washington DC 20036

State:
1. Florida Association for Media in Education (FAME)
    P. O. Box 13119
    Tallahassee FL 32308

Local:

1. Local affiliates of state organizations such as FAME
2. Public library support groups

Related Organizations

National:
1. National Education Association (NEA)
    1201 North Street NW
    Washington DC 20036-3290
2. American Federation of Teachers (AFT)
    555 New Jersey Avenue, NW
    Washington DC 20001-2079
3. Phi Delta Kappa International, Inc.
    408 N. Union
    P. O. Box 789
    Bloomington IN 47402
4. International Reading Association
    800 Barksdale Road
    Newark DE 19711-3269

5. Association of Supervision and Curriculum Development (ASCD)
   1250 N. Pitt Street
   Alexandria VA 22314-1453

State / Local:

1. State / Local affiliates of NEA
2. State / Local affiliates of AFT

DOE 24.1   18, 40, 48

SKILL 1.9 Identify professional development sources and certification requirements.

Professional development resources are extensive in scope as evidenced by the resource list in this guide.

Other sources include the college and university programs offered at many state and private institutions. Degrees in library science, information science, or educational media are offered for both undergraduates and graduate students. Some universities offer extern programs or on-line courses.

Workshops are offered at state conferences and through district inservice programs.

State Certification requirements adopted in 1992 offer two plans:

1. a bachelor's or higher degree with an undergraduate or graduate major in educational media.
2. a bachelor's or higher degree with thirty (30) semester hours in educational media.

DOE 24.3   18, 40

COMPETENCY 2.0 UNDERSTANDING THE PROFESSIONAL ISSUES CONCERNING LIBRARY MEDIA CENTERS.

SKILL 2.1 Identify the principles of intellectual freedom.

The principles of intellectual freedom are guaranteed by the First Amendment to the Constitution of the United States. They are reinforced in the Library Bill of Rights adapted by the ALA in 1948, the AECT's statement on intellectual freedom (1978), the freedom to read and review statements of the ALA (1953 and 1979), and the National Council of English Teachers, Students Right to Read Statement.

The principles as they relate to children:
1. Freedom of access to information in all formats through activities that develop critical thinking and problem solving skills.
2. Freedom of access to ideas that present a variety of points of view through activities that teach discriminating reading.
3. Freedom to acquire information reflective of the intellectual, physical, and social growth of the user.

It becomes the responsibility of the school library media specialist to develop and maintain a collection development policy (4.6.1) that ensures these freedoms.

DOE 25.1   3, 26, 38, 41, 45, 48

SKILL 2.2 Describe an ethically appropriate course of action regarding a challenge to intellectual freedom.

Despite the best collection development policies, an occasional complaint will arise. In our society the following issues cause controversy: politics, gay rights, profanity, pornography, creationism vs. evolution, the occult, sex education, racism and violence. Adults disagree philosophically about these issues. They will often express their concern first to the school library media specialist. Ethically, he is bound to protect the principles of intellectual freedom, but he is also bound by those same principles to treat the complaint seriously as the expression of an opposing view.

The most important thing is not to panic. The challenge is not an affront to the media specialist but a complaint about the content, language, or graphics in a material. The first step is to greet the complainant calmly and explain the principles of intellectual freedom you are bound to uphold. A good paraphrase from the AECT Statement is that a learner's right to access information can only be abridged by an agreement between parent and child. With the current emphasis on the V chip for selective television viewing, parents are becoming more aware of their own roles in censoring unwanted images from their children. In most instances, a calm, rational discussion will satisfy the challenger.

However, if the challenge is pursued, the media specialist will have to follow district procedures for handling the complaint. The appropriate school administrator should be informed. Of course, an administrator may have been confronted initially. In either instance the complainant is asked to fill out a formal complaint form, citing his specific objection in a logical manner. Sometimes, simply thinking the issue through clearly and recognizing that someone will truly listen to his complaint is enough of a solution. If all else fails, a reconsideration committee should be appointed to take the matter under advisement and recommend a course of action.

DOE 27.2   3, 25, 38, 41, 4

SKILL 2.3 Examine and apply copyright laws appropriately.

The advent of technology that made copying print and non-print media efficient poses serious concern for educators who unwittingly or otherwise violate copyright law on a regular basis. Regardless of their intentions to provide their students access to materials that may be too costly for mass purchase, educators must understand the reasons for copyright protection and they must, by example, ensure the upholding of that protection.

There are many fine publications which clarify copyright law for educators. In many instances, school districts endorse these publications or provide their own concise summarizes for reference. Though all educators should be cognizant of the law, it becomes the responsibility of the school library media specialist to help inform colleagues and monitor the proper application of the law.

Actually, educators have the benefit of greater leeway in copying than any other group. Many print instructional materials carry statements that allow production of multiple copies for classroom use, provided they adhere to the "Guidelines for Classroom Copying in Nonprofit Educational Institutions." Teachers may duplicate enough copies to provide one per student per course provided that they meet the tests of brevity, spontaneity, and cumulative effect.

1. Brevity test:

    Poetry - suggested maximum 250 words.

    Prose - one complete essay, story, or article less than 2500 words or excerpts of no more than 1000 words or 10% of the work, whichever is less. (Children's books with text under 2500 words may not be copied in their entirety. No more than two pages containing 10% of the text may be copied.)

    Illustration - charts, drawings, cartoons, etc. are limited to one per book or periodical article.

2. Spontaneity test:

    Normally copying that does not fall under the brevity test requires publisher's permission for duplication. However, allowances are made if "the inspiration and decision to use the work" occur too soon prior to classroom use for permission to be sought in writing.

3. Cumulative effect test:

    Even in the case of short poems or prose, it is preferable to make only one copy. However, three short items from one work are allowable during one class term. Reuse of copied material from term to term is expressly forbidden. Compilation of works into anthologies to be used in place of purchasing texts is prohibited.

Copyright legislation has existed in the United States for more than 100 years. Conflicts over copyright were settled in the courts. The 1976 Copyright Act, especially section 107 dealing with Fair Use, created legislative criteria to follow based on judicial precedents. In 1978, when the law took effect, it set regulations for duration and scope of copyright, specified author rights, and set monetary penalties for infringement. The statutory penalty may be waived by the court for an employee of a non-profit educational institution where the employee can prove fair use intent.

Fair use, especially important to educators, is meant to create a balance between copyright protection and the needs of learners for access to protected material. Fair use is judged by the purpose of the use, the nature of the work (whether creative or informational), the quantity of the work for use, and the market effect. In essence, if a portion of a work is used to benefit the learner with no intent to deprive the author of his profits, fair use is granted. Recently, Fair Use has been challenged most in cases of videotaping off-air of television programs. Guidelines too numerous to delineate here affect copying audio-visual materials and computer software. Most distributors place written regulations in the packaging of these products. Allowances for single back-up copies in the event of damage to the original are granted.

Section 108 is pertinent to libraries in that it permits reproducing a single copy of an entire work if no financial gain is derived, if the library is public or archival, and if the copyright notice appears on all copies.

In any event in which violation of the law is a concern, the safest course of action is to seek written permission from the publisher of the copyrighted work. If permission is granted, a copy of that permission should accompany any duplicates.

DOE 27.1   25, 41, 48

SKILL 2.4 Describe an ethically appropriate course of action regarding a violation of copyright.

When a suspected infringement of copyright is brought to the attention of the school library media specialist, she should follow certain procedures.
1. Determine if a violation has in effect occurred. Never accuse or report alleged instances to a higher authority without verification.
2. If an instance is verified, tactfully inform the violator of the specific criteria to use so that future violations can be avoided. Presented properly, the information will be accepted as constructive.
3. If advise is unheeded and further infractions occur, bring them to the attention of the teacher's supervisor - a team leader or

department chair - who can handle the matter as an evaluation procedure.

4. Inform the person who has reported the alleged violation of the procedures being used.

DOE NA

SKILL 2.5 Examine the issue of flexible access.

The issue of flexible access is especially distressing to elementary school library media specialists who are placed in the "related arts wheel," providing planning time for art, music, and physical education teachers. "Closed" or rigid scheduling, i.e. scheduling classes to meet regularly for instruction in the library, prohibits the implementation of the integrated program philosophy essential to the principles of intellectual freedom.

The AASL Position Statement on Flexible Scheduling asserts that schools must adopt a philosophy of full integration of library media into the total educational program. This integration assures a partnership of students, teachers, and school library media specialists in the use of readily accessible materials and services when they are appropriate to the classroom curriculum.

All parties in the school community - teachers, principal, district administration, and school board - must share the responsibility for contributing to flexible access.

Research on the validity of flexible access reinforces the need for cooperative planning with teachers, an objective that cannot be met if the school library media specialist has no time for the required planning sessions. Rigid scheduling denies students the freedom to come to the library during the school day for pleasurable reading and self-motivated inquiry activities vital to the development of critical thinking, problem solving, and exploratory skills. Without flexible access, the library becomes just another self-contained classroom.

DOE 25.3   8, 14, 41

SKILL 2.6 Examine judicial rulings that have impacted library media issues.

Judicial rulings have come in the area of copyright issues. The 1975 ruling in the case of Williams & Wilkins Co. v. U.S. provided guidance to legislators in preparing the fair use provisions of the 1976 Copyright Act. It ruled that entire articles may be mass-duplicated for use which advances the public welfare without doing economic harm to the publishers. This ruling provides encouragement to educators that fair use may be interpreted more liberally.

In 1984, the ruling in the Sony Corp. of America v. Universal City Studios, Inc. placed the burden of proving infringement on the plaintiff. The Supreme Court upheld the right of individuals to off-air videotape television programs for non-commercial use. Thus, a copyright holder must prove that the use of videotaped programming is intentionally harmful. Civil suits against educators would require the plaintiff to prove that the existing or potential market would be negatively affected by use of these programs in a classroom setting.

Current fair use practice specifies that a videotaped copy must be shown within 10 days of its airing and be kept no longer than 45 days for use in constructing supplemental teaching materials related to the programming.

Court rulings have ambiguously addressed the issue of censorship. In 1972, the U.S. Court of Appeals for the Second Circuit (President's Council v. Community School Board No. 25, New York City) ruled in favor of the removal of a library book, reasoning that its removal did not oppose or aid religion.

In 1976, the Court of Appeals for the Sixth Circuit (Minarcini v. Strongsville City School District) ruled against the removal of Joseph Heller's Catch 22 and two Kurt Vonnequt novels on the grounds that removal of books from a school library is a burden on the freedom of classroom discussion and an infringement of the First Amendment's guarantee of an individual's "right to know."

A Massachusetts district court (Right to Read Defense Committee v. School Board of the City of Chelsea) ordered the school board to return to the high school library a poetry anthology which contained "objectionable and filthy" language. The court asserted that the school had control over curriculum but not library collections.

Three cases in the 1980's dealt with challenging the removal of materials from high school libraries. The first two, in circuit courts, condemned the burning of banned books (Zykan v. Warsaw Community School Corporation, Indiana) and the removal of books of considerable literary merit. The case of Board of Education, Island Trees Union Free School District 26 (New York) v. Pico reached the Supreme Court in 1982 after the U.S. Court of Appeals for the Second Circuit had reversed a lower court ruling granting the school board the right to remove nine books which had been deemed "anti-American, anti-Semitic, anti-Christian and just plain filthy." The Supreme Court in a 5-4 ruling upheld the Court of Appeals' ruling and the nine books were returned. The dissenting opinion, however, continued to foster ambiguity claiming that, if the intent was to deny free access to ideas, it was an infringement of the First Amendment, but if the intent was to remove pervasively vulgar material, the board had just cause. Ultimately, the issue hinged on a school board's authority in determining the selection of optional rather than required reading. Library books, being optional, should not be denied to users.

DOE 25.2   3, 25, 36, 41, 48

COMPETENCY 3.0 UNDERSTANDING THE SCHOOL LIBRARY MEDIA SPECIALIST'S ROLE.

Diverse, ever-changing, and always challenging, the role of the school library media specialist is a pivotal one. Always the teacher and information specialist, she has in the last twenty years experienced a role expansion unparalleled in education, not only because of the advancing technology but also because of the need for her to assume a leadership responsibility in the school community.

SKILL 3.1 Recognize role as instructor.

3.1.1 Identify instructional responsibilities for student patrons.

Despite the diversity of responsibilities, a school library media specialist is first and foremost a teacher. The percentage of time devoted to structured teaching activities is greater in elementary school, especially if the media center is still on rigid scheduling. As students mature, structured lessons should be shortened and followed by longer hands-on activities for reinforcement of the learned skills.

Several factors have contributed to defining the school library media specialist's instructional role.

1. Introduction of pre-kindergarten programs into elementary schools. As more public schools have introduced PK programs, many states have expanded certification parameters. However, training in understanding that age group and its unique needs have not kept pace. One survey indicated that most certified media specialists considered parenthood their best qualification for dealing with preschoolers.
2. Greater emphasis on developing higher order thinking skills. Even in primary grades, students are encouraged to synthesize information and make media productions to present the results of their learning. Middle school students should be reading critically and making value judgments about the quality of their reading material.
3. Cooperative planning and learning. Research affirms that information skills instruction must be integrated into the curriculum. Furthermore, the days of silence in libraries has

given way to learning noise, students working in groups with the necessary communication. Working in teams gives the students preparation for the real work world.

At all levels, library media specialists should be expected to
1. Train students in information location using traditional and new information retrieval skills.
2. Facilitate students' understanding of different media formats and the purpose of various information presentation formats.
3. Assist students in developing critical thinking skills in relation to the located information.
4. Reinforce library media citizenship skills.
5. Teach information skills.

DOE 1.1   1, 15, 22, 35, 49, 51

3.1.2 Use local and state information skills' scope and sequence to plan lesson development appropriate to specific grade/ability levels.

In 1984, the School Library Media Services Section of the Florida DOE produced *Information Skills for Florida Schools K-12* which set guidelines for the acquisition of information skills. In grade level groupings, skills were identified in six areas: orientation, organization, selection and utilization, comprehension and application, presentation of information, and appreciation. Basic skills are identified at the grade level for appropriate introduction. Then, objectives are specified at each successive level to review, reinforce, or expand those skills.

For example, the skill of organization dealing with the card catalog is introduced in Grade Levels K-2 as the ability to identify the location and purpose of the card catalog. In Grade Levels 3-4 the skill is expanded to identify the arrangement of and locate information in the card catalog. Grade Levels 5-6 require applying filing rules to locating materials, Grade Levels 7-8 require recognizing using added entry cards, and Grade Levels 9-12 require identifying different catalog formats and classification systems.

(Since most schools have gone to automated cataloging in recent years, identification and use of automated formats should be integrated into the continuum.)

The wording of some skills remain the same in all levels. Examples include those concerning selection and use of equipment and accessories and organizing and presenting information/ideas by designing/producing materials. The types of equipment and material change from filmstrip and finger puppets in K-2 to advanced video equipment and research papers in 9-12. The skill is introduced in K-2 and reviewed, reinforced, and expanded at subsequent grade levels. Using appropriate sources to locate information is introduced at Grade Levels 3-4 with using dictionaries, encyclopedias, and telephone directories; expanded to include atlases, almanacs, periodicals, etc. at Grade Levels 5-6; indexes, yearbooks, specialized dictionaries at Grade Levels 7-8; and handbooks, thesauri, computerized references, and government documents at Grade Levels 9-12.

Some skills are introduced and appear at only one level: identifying the concept of intellectual freedom is introduced as an appreciation skill in Grades 7-8.

Some districts adopt or adapt this DOE scope and sequence according to student ability levels, availability of resources, and other program or facility factors. Each school library media specialist must determine where her students are in sequence prior to planning a teaching strategy.

DOE 1.2   14, 18, 50, 51

3.1.3 Incorporate information skills into curriculum.

This objective can be best achieved if there are existing scope and sequences in other curricular areas. Information skills, like any other content, should not be taught in isolation if they are to be retained and practiced. If no printed sequentials exist, consult with teachers and/or team leaders about planning activities cooperatively to teach information and content skills concurrently.

Teaming with teachers will also meet their instructional objectives. Media specialists need to match resources to those objectives as well as suggest means for using media to demonstrate student skills mastery. Achievement of the design of resource-based teaching units with supplemental or total involvement of the library media center resources and services satisfy levels 9 and 10 of Loertscher's eleven level taxonomy, which assumes the active involvement of the school library media specialist in the total school program.

Finally, the self-esteem of students and teachers who learn information management skills is as significant as the information acquisition.

A suggested procedure for incorporation follows:

Preparation:
1. Secure any printed scope and sequences from content areas.
2. Meet with team leaders or department chairs early in the year to plan an integrated, sequential program.
3. Attend department or grade-level meetings with specific time devoted to orienting teachers to available resources and services. Plan best time to schedule orientations for entry level students and reviews for reinforcement.

Implementation:
1. Conduct planned lessons. Distribute copies of objectives, activities, and resources.
2. Review search strategies and challenge students to broaden scope of resources used to locate information.
3. Provide adequate time for students to carry out lesson activities using media center resources.

Evaluation:
1. Solicit feedback from both students and teachers.
2. Incorporate suggestions into lesson plans.

DOE 1.3   14, 35, 51, 52

3.1.4 Identify media formats to satisfy specific learning needs.
Many teachers today would be surprised to learn that videotape
is not always the best instruction format. Fourth Grade
students studying mollusks and their structures can be shown
how to make their own color-lift transparencies. In a high
school biology class, the teacher may use a personally
designed laser disk lesson to introduce a unit on microscopic
organisms that affect biodegradation before students use the
electron microscope.

After reading a story to her kindergarten class, the teacher may
have students design and create their own puppets of the
characters using paper bags while the Third Grade teacher
using a similar lesson might expect the students to make a
slide-tape presentation using a 35 mm camera, a copy stand,
and an audio-cassette recorder. Either format will allow the
students to exhibit their comprehension of the plot and
characters in each story. (See 3.4.2 for additional information.)

DOE 1.4   7, 50

3.1.5 Identify activities that enrich students' reading, viewing,
listening, and production skills.

To follow the skills progression in the various taxonomies of
learning skills, a series of activities is suggested.
1. Recall expects the ability to retell a story in proper
sequence and to identify the characters and places where
the events occur. School library media specialists can
suggest titles of books, filmstrips or videotapes appropriate
for each user's ability and interest. Young students can
exhibit recall mastery by orally retelling the story,
dramatizing the story through role play, and drawing
pictures or making puppets of the characters. Mature
students can develop a story board and create slides or
videotapes of their own reenactment. PK-2 students should
be expected to recall a list of instructions and act on them.
Training them in the use of location, retrieval, and circulation
procedures will enhance their listening skills so they can
become productive media center users.
2. Comprehension. Students in upper primary grades exhibit
the ability to explain the main idea of a passage or the
theme of a story. Reading, listening, and viewing can be

enhanced by outlining the main points of a written passage, audiotape or record, and any of the visual media: filmstrips, slides, videotapes, laser disks. At this level, they can produce slides, transparencies, posters, or models that demonstrate their understanding of the material. They can show the cause/effect relationship of happenings by discussing and practicing the behavioral procedures required to work cooperatively in the media center.

3. Inference. After reading a story/book, listening to a record or audiotape, or viewing a filmstrip or videotape, a middle school student should be able to interpret character actions, determine the logic of plot sequences, relate knowledge from the reading to real life, and infer information about characters from dialogue. They might predict a new course of action, were a given event to change. Some middle school and most high school students should be able to orally discuss inferences after reading, viewing, or listening to most media formats. Students at this point can learn to discriminate the appearance and function of various media formats and match them to appropriate learning activities. Students at this level may also be encouraged to study television production, photography or related media arts. Students may be planning and producing daily announcements via closed circuit television.

4. Evaluation. Secondary students now judge the quality and appropriateness of reading materials, making selections independently. They can be expected to assess the quality of the author's writing style, the effectiveness of character and plot development, the bias of the writer's/producer's presentation, and the appropriateness of the language used to convey information. Students at this level should master concentrated listening skills by taking study notes from printed matter, lectures, or audio-visual programs. Learning should not only result in written research papers but in audio-visual projects. Students should be taught design, production, and editing skills.

5. Appreciation. Accomplishable in varying degrees at every level is the ability to express an emotional response to subject matter or a reaction to the author's language or a movie's theme or graphic detail. Younger students' reactions will be observable immediately. Requests for more of the same will keep the media specialist searching for similar materials. Older youngsters can be expected to

write appraisals that incorporate evaluation and appreciation skills. Those with definite, vocal opinions may be encouraged to serve on the library media advisory committee.

DOE 2.1   25, 36, 46, 50

3.1.6 Identify evaluation methods for reading, viewing, listening, or production skills.

1. Students' reading habits can be evaluated by use of student surveys or interviews, by packaged assessment programs like Accelerated Reader, or by some in-house record keeping system. Several good standardized tests exist for testing reading progression.

2. Visual literacy can be evaluated by observing students' own visual designs - from drawings, graphic designs, and photographs to motion pictures and computer graphics. Students must also be able to verbally analyze various images they perceive and to interpret the messages delivered.

3. Listening skills are evaluated by observing the student's ability to follow oral directions, to remember facts and details, and to retell a series of pieces of information. Standardized or teacher-made tests can pre-test and post-test listening skills mastery.

4. Media literacy is evaluated by observing students' use of equipment needed to create productions and noting the final product of media projects for appropriateness of format, length and depth of coverage, graphic quality, focus, etc. (3.4.2)

DOE 2.5   7, 24, 30, 46, 51

3.1.7 Identify techniques for motivating students to apply, interpret and evaluate various media.

Motivational techniques are derived from child development needs. Obviously, students must receive personal satisfaction from any pursuit, but some students for whom the reward of pleasure is not enough must have other stimulants.

Some motivational techniques:
1. The classroom teacher's approval of using different media as an integral part of learning. Students will emulate the opinions and practices of persons they respect. Involve the teachers, and the students will follow. However, the media used should be current and appropriate to the learning needs.
2. The availability of current equipment which is in good condition. Many students have computers and video equipment in their own homes. Sometimes the quality of their equipment and their skill in using it exceeds that of the school. Students want to experiment with emerging technologies and create quality productions.
3. External rewards. Producing media for graded class projects or contests, being asked to preview media for its appropriateness for classroom use or helping to develop products that will be seen by parent or community groups will encourage student involvement.

DOE 2.6   7, 24, 30

3.1.8 Identify techniques for the establishment of lifelong learning habits.

Students need to know the variety of information resources and agencies available to them and be given frequent opportunities to use them in order to establish habit. By learning about the resources available outside the school, they will more likely pursue using these services in adulthood.

1. Inform them of resource sharing networks - public and academic libraries, Internet services, and community agencies - that provide information. Some schools in districts with fully automated public library systems may provide on-line access to the public library catalog from a terminal at the school site. Public libraries also offer on-line cataloging services that can be accessed from home computers and some are now providing access to the

Internet. Some schools subscribe to on-line services such as *America On Line* or *CompuServe*.

In 1992 the Florida Department of Education's School Media Services Division introduced SUNLINK, a CD-ROM union database, which facilitates interlibrary loan throughout the state's public schools. Each project school was provided funds in 1995-96 to purchase a dedicated computer for the SUNLINK program.

Community colleges and universities encourage high school students to share their facilities for information gathering.

2. Invite representatives from other information agencies to promote their programs through the schools. Post public library hours, advertisements of lectures, book reviews, or other library activities; arrange for guest speakers from Internet providers or radio and television stations; and participate in field trips to other information centers.

DOE 2.7   45, 49, 50

SKILL 3.2 Recognize role of staff development consultant.

3.2.1 Identify methods of educating staff in the selection, production, use, and evaluation of media.

Staff, including teachers and support personnel, should be offered periodic in-service in learning new skills and reinforcing known skills. These skills may be taught at formal, structured workshops or in informal small-group or individual sessions when a need arises.

1. A hands-on orientation for teachers new to school - to familiarize them with available resource and equipment and apprise them of services - should include information on incorporating appropriate media into their lessons. Written procedures for selection and evaluation should be available (4.6.4 - 4.6.6). Use a variety of media formats in presenting the information - overhead transparencies or LED projections for lists and forms; a videotape program on producing transparencies, slides, videotape, etc.; the automated card catalog for search procedures.

2. Provide information on new/existing media and solicit recommendations.
   a. Send bibliographies, catalogs, or newsletters frequently, asking for purchase suggestions.
   b. Inform all teachers of district and school preview policies and arrange previews for purchase suggestions.
   c. Involve as many teachers as possible on review committees (3.3.2).

3. Provide periodic brief refresher modules. Advertise the media and equipment to be used in each session. Suggest uses of each lesson's media format so teachers can make appropriate choices. Have teachers create one or more products at each session that can be used for instruction in an upcoming lesson.

4. Secure oral or written feedback on both teacher-made and commercial media used in classroom lessons. Ask them to use appropriate evaluation criteria (3.4.3) in measuring the product's worth. The more familiar they become with the criteria the better their product choices will become.

DOE 4.1   7, 18, 24

3.2.2 Identify the elements of a staff development activity in the effective use of media and equipment.

Designing a staff development activity follows a basic lesson profile with special considerations for adult learners.
1. Analyze learner styles. Adult learners are more receptive to role playing and individual performance before a group. Learner motivation is more internal, but some external motivations, such as release time, compensatory time, inservice credit or some written recognition, might be discussed with the principal.
2. Assess learner needs. Survey teachers to determine which media or equipment they want to learn more about. Consider environmental factors - time, place, temperature. Since many inservice activities occur after school, taking the lesson to the teachers in their own classrooms may make them more comfortable especially if they can have a reviving afternoon snack. If they must come to the media center, serve refreshments.
3. Select performance objectives. Determine exactly what the teacher should be able to do at the end of a successful inservice session.
4. Plan activities to achieve objectives. Demonstrate the skill to be taught, involve the participants in active performance/ production, and allow for practice and feedback.
5. Select appropriate resources. Arrange that all materials and equipment are ready and in good functioning order on the day of the inservice.
6. Determine instructor. Either the school library media specialist or a faculty member should conduct these on-site inservices unless the complexity or novelty of the technology requires an outside expert.

7. Provide continuing support. The instructor or designated substitute should be available after the inservice for reinforcement.
8. Evaluation. Determine the effectiveness of the inservice and make modifications as recommended in future inservices.

DOE 4.2   38, 41, 47

3.2.3 Identify approaches to updating staff about the uses of emerging technologies.

Because we are in the business of teaching, all technologies must be viewed as educational tools. To enable teachers to understand the way these technologies can be applied in their classrooms, they must understand the relationship between these tools and learning needs. The school library media professionals must be able to update teachers on this correlation.
1. Conduct timely, short inservice activities to demonstrate and allow teachers to manipulate new technologies and plan classroom uses.
2. Clip articles or write reviews to distribute to teachers with suggestions for application in their particular learning environment.
3. Offer to plan and teach lessons in different content areas.

DOE 4.3   24, 41, 45

SKILL 3.3 Recognize role as information specialist.

3.3.1 Exhibit knowledge of methods and resources to use in response to a reference request or a specific information need.

Reference requests are of three types depending on the depth of the question and the scope of the search. Some very simple questions can lead to complex searches, however.
1. Ready reference request. These requests usually require a limited search in standard reference books (encyclopedias, atlases, almanacs, etc.) or electronic databases (SIRS Researcher, Grolier's Encyclopedia, 3D Atlas, or American Heritage Dictionary and Thesaurus). The request is

satisfied by directing the requestor to the exact sources in which the information may be found. Occasionally, a seemingly simple question cannot be answered quickly and thus necessitates a higher level search.

A request for the names of the current governor and cabinet can be found easily in *The Florida Handbook* or *Taylor's Encyclopedia of Government Officials*. However, a request for biographical information about an obscure or subject-specific person may require delving into many biographical dictionaries or encyclopedias.

If the library carries the *Who's Who in America* and *Who Was Who in America* series, an American is easy to identify. However, most school library media centers do not purchase biographical dictionaries of foreign persons unless they were noteworthy in a particular profession. *Who's Who in Science, Current Biography, Webster's Biographical Dictionary, British Writers Before 1900,* etc. are some helpful resources.

2. Specific need requests. These requests are the most frequently addressed and may range from merely steering the requestor to a card catalog, index, or other bibliographic aid if the user is familiar with those tools or may become a lengthy project if the resource must be found outside the school or if the user needs instruction in using search tools and locating the resources.

A student debater may want to know which resources would give statistics about teen pregnancy. A teacher may ask which books and periodicals have the best articles on inclusion of special education students.

The answer to specific need questions entails locating the resources by identifying the proper search tools (card catalog, the *Reader's Guide to Periodical Literature*, or automated indexes like Infotrac or Newsbank).

3. Research request. This question is encountered most often in secondary school or university/academic libraries. The search is broader in scope and requires more time. Any specific need request could be expanded into a research request.

The debater may be preparing a portfolio for contest and need photocopies of available material. A teacher taking a college course may ask the school library media specialist to pull periodical articles relating to inclusion. These requests may require using on-line databases and research queries outside the library media center.

Research services are gaining wider need as users are confronted with great amounts of information and less time to conduct their searches.

DOE 6.1, 6.2   29

3.3.2 Identify resource selection methods.

Selecting appropriate materials requires a knowledge of the resource tools.

1. Companies who offer collection lists designed for elementary, middle, or secondary schools or for special content schools - vocational or performing arts. These lists are used most often for opening a new school library media center. School library media specialists and review committees customize these lists to user needs.

2. Publisher's catalogs. These are good starting points for locating specific titles and comparison shopping.

3. Vendors representing one or more publishers. Too little has been said about establishing good relationships with vendors, who have access to demonstration materials and can make them available for review. Naturally, they want to sell their employers' products; however, most are familiar with their competitors' product lines and work collaboratively to help schools secure the most appropriate materials.

4. Review publications. *School Library Journal* and *Booklist* offer concise reviews on current books. *Children and Books* [resource #45] contains a thorough list of book selection aids. *Technology Review, New Media,* and other media/ computer magazines offer evaluation of audio-visual and computer software and hardware.

5. Bibliographic indexes of subject specific titles with summaries. These indexes are not free and are most cost effective if housed in the district professional library. The same is true of *Books in Print*, in print and non-print formats. Because its contents change significantly from year to year, many districts cannot justify its cost, relying instead on direct communication with publishers to determine a book's status.

Methods:
1. Review resources using existing tools.

   The school library media center staff should gather information concerning contents and cost of considered items and budget allocation figures.

2. Organize a review committee. This may be a district committee for selection of materials to be purchased for several schools or a local committee (the library media advisory committee if one exists) for selection of specific titles or series. The committee should be comprised mainly of teachers, representing a cross-section of grade levels and subject areas.

   At the district review, involving large numbers of items, the district supervisor may have items available for on-site preview. If possible, the school committee should have products available for examination. Ask a vendor to make a presentation.

3. Use the material in a classroom setting for an immediate evaluation of its worth. Naturally, this method requires that a faculty member - teacher or library media specialist - preview the item first to determine its suitability for the intended audience.

Preferably, written records of all reviews should be kept in the district media office. Most districts have a preview form for rating an item against evaluative criteria (4.6.5).

DOE 5.1   7, 18, 48

3.3.3 Identify the elements of an effective resource organization system.

Resource organization systems vary from school to school, based on factors such as user demand, storage considerations, staff limitations and preferences, and processing procedures. Some media specialists separate specific age/reading level collections for ease of location, especially with younger children. Audio-visual and multi-media kits may be shelved with print material if they can be circulated to all users. Visibility creates greater use. However, collection security for instructional materials and equipment must also be considered. Organizational procedures should be logical and follow standardized procedures as much as possible.

The objective of organization systems:
1. Ready access. To make resources, regardless of format, easy to locate, a bibliographic control system must be in place. A catalog, preferably automated, should include all print and non-print resources and equipment. *Florida School Media Programs: A Guide for Excellence* recommends that all school-owned media should appear in the media center catalog regardless of where they housed.
2. Circulation ease. If the card catalog is not automated, the media center staff should keep accurate circulation records to facilitate retrieval and inventory. If audio-visual materials or equipment are not housed near the circulation area, a paper record is necessary. For equipment not housed in the media center itself, location information must appear in the catalog.

DOE 5.2   1, 18

3.3.4 Identify resource sharing concepts and systems.

Resource sharing has always been an integral part of education. Before the technology revolution, the sharing was done within schools or departments and between teachers. Now it is possible to access information around the world.

Resource sharing is a way of
1. Providing a broader information base to enable users to find and access the resources that provide the needed information.
2. Reducing or containing media center budgets.
3. Establishing cooperation with other resource providers that encourage mutual planning and standardization of control.

Resource sharing systems:
1. Interlibrary loan. The advent of computer databases has simplified the process of locating sources in other libraries.
   a. Local public library collections can be accessed from terminals in the media center. Physical access depends on going to the branch where the material is housed.
   b. SUNLINK (3.1.8) will eventually convert all public school collections to a CD-ROM database. There is a provision for borrowing from the general collections of participating schools. Materials are borrowed and returned by mail.

2. Networking systems.
   a. FIRN (Florida Information Resources Network) is an on-line service available free to all active public school teachers. FIRN provides special databases of educational services from the DOE or other state agencies as well as access to the World Wide Web. E-mail allows educators to communicate across the state.
   b. On-line services (Internet providers) offer access to a specific menu of locations. Monthly fees and/or time charges must be budgeted.
   c. Individual city or county network systems. These are community sponsored networks, often part of the public library system, which provides Internet access for the price of a local phone call. A time limit usually confines an individual search to allow more users access.

    d. On-line continuing education programs offer courses/
degrees through at-home study. Large school districts
provide lessons for homebound students or home school
advocates.

    e. Bulletin boards allow individuals or groups to converse
electronically with persons in another place. Students in
Florida and Nicaragua can share study activities.

3. Telecommunications. Using telephone and television as the
media for communication, telecommunications is used
primarily for distance learning. Universities or networks of
universities (University of South Carolina and a consortium
in North Carolina) provide workshops, conferences, and
college credit courses for educators as well as courses for
senior high school students in subjects that could not
generate adequate class counts in their home schools.
Large school districts offer broadcast programming for
homebound/home school students.

The advantage is that students are provided with a phone
number so they can interact with the instructors or
information providers.

DOE 5.4, 5.5   7, 18, 41, 49

SKILL 3.4 Recognize role as materials production consultant.

3.4.1 Determine need for which products must be designed and executed.

In the last twenty years, audio-visual materials, once considered supplementary to instruction, have become instructional media, integral parts of the instructional process. Students and teachers should learn not only to use commercial products but to design and produce their own materials.

It is appropriate for faculty to produce their own resources when
1. Commercial products are unavailable, unsuited to learning styles/preferences/environments, or too costly.
2. Teaching styles indicate a preference for non-commercial products.
3. Teachers have the expertise and necessary equipment for original production.

It is appropriate for students to produce their own resources when
1. Achieving understanding with non-verbal means of expression.
2. Communicating ideas and information to others.
3. Expressing creativity.
4. Demonstrating mastery of lesson objectives by alternative means.

DOE 3.1   7, 24, 30

3.4.2 Determine media formats and resources required in the design and production to meet a specific instructional need.

Having determined that it is appropriate to use teacher or student/produced media, it is necessary to determine which media should be produced to meet the specific instructional need. School library media specialists may produce media for two purposes:
1. To make presentations for information skills instruction, other teacher-directed activities, or testing.
2. To make materials to be placed directly in the hands of students.

Many excellent books on media instruction detail the instructional uses of media formats. A few will be summarized here.

1. Introduction. Formats that allow large group listening or viewing are appropriate for introducing new materials: filmstrips, films, slidetapes, computer projection, overhead transparencies, and videotapes (require large screen, elevation of monitor, or multiple units). With young learners display boards with large print and audiocassettes for story-telling with non-readers are most effective.

2. Application. During this phase, media that lend themselves to individual or small group use are needed. As students Investigate the subject matter, organize that information, practice, or demonstrate understanding, they may create any or several types of media. With young children these would include manipulatives - building blocks, letters or numbers, or shapes - in cloth, plastic, or wood. Older students would create photographs/slides, audiocassette tapes, or videotapes. Some secondary students might even design their own computer programs. Students at all levels can be taught to use computer design software to create multi-media productions.

The application of media production techniques helps the producer - adult or child - clarify his own objectives and determine the exact format which would best present his ideas and achieve his goals. A lesson on distinguishing the calls of local birds might use audiocassette tape while recognizing plumage would use slides or videotape. Students preparing a study of estaurine ecology might incorporate video and computer graphics designed from electron microscope imagery to demonstrate types of micro-organisms in the local river.

DOE 3.2   7, 24, 30, 47

3.4.3 Identify methods of planning , designing, and evaluating media.

Once the determination to produce media has been made, there is a process for planning, designing, and evaluating the product.

Planning:
1. State the main idea (goal) of the production, clearly and concisely.
2. Determine the purpose of the product.
    a. To provide information or develop appreciation. Media with this purpose is general in nature, usually meant for presentation to a class or larger group, and involves the audience as passive listeners. However, it must use dramatic or motivational appeals to hold audience interest.
    b. To provide instruction. Designed for individual or small group use, instructive media should be specific, systematic, and interactive.
3. Develop the objectives. State specifically what the audience should know or be able to do after using this media and what measurements will be used to determine their knowledge or ability.
4. Analyze the audience. Determine ability and interest, learning styles, and current understanding of the topic.
5. Research the idea. Use print, non-print, and human resources to study both the subject matter and the media techniques/formats to best present the subject matter.

Designing:
1. Prepare an outline of the content. Create story board cards for each subheading and match them to the objectives.
2. Select the media format(s) to communicate your idea. Consider time, effort, and cost as well as audio-visual needs. If motion or sound are not essential, consider using transparencies or slides which are easier to make and require no editing. Consider the equipment and facilities available.
3. Create the content. Prepare a story board delineating the description of each graphic and write a corresponding script if captions or sound narration will be included.
4. Create the media (3.4.4).

Evaluating:
1. Observe reaction of audience to resources. Body language and verbal reactions, especially in younger children, will indicate the level of interest.

2. Solicit verbal or written reactions to appearance, arrangement, and technical quality as well as ease of understanding and mastery of content.
3. Examine costs. Determine if costs of materials and time invested were equal to outcomes.

DOE 3.3   7, 24, 30

3.4.4 Identify techniques of producing various media formats.

Specific methods of producing graphic, photographic, audio, video and computer media are dealt with extensively in the resources cited. However, generally production of media formats involve the need to

1. Determine display format - easel or wall board, poster, hand-out, transparency, videotape, etc.
2. Plan art work - lettering font, size, margin, mount, visual layout, color/shading, lighting, etc.
3. Select materials - paper, laminating film, photographic film, etc.
4. Select production equipment - calligraphy pens, copy stand, camera, opaque projector, letter press, etc.
5. Complete the process following plan/storyboard. Letter, draw, photograph, shoot film, merge graphics/text, etc.
6. Organize and edit. Put display in order, set slides in tray, dub audio track to edited videotape. Plan time for recreating any art work with technical flaws.
7. Package the product. Mount transparencies, laminate posters, photocopy hand-outs, add credits, etc.

DOE 3.4   7, 24, 30

SKILL 3.5 Recognize role as technologist.

3.5.1 Provide training for students and teachers in the use of available technologies.

School library media specialists have always been responsible for instructing students and teachers in the use of equipment and the media used with them.

Now they must also teach both teachers and students how to use computers and their applications. If the media center has only computers for the automated catalog, the instruction is usually done for individuals or small groups as they need to locate materials. Peer instruction can be very efficient in using automated indexes. Student library aides or volunteers can assist with informal instruction.

If the media center has an attached computer lab, operation of and instruction in the lab may also become his responsibility. Support staff or paraprofessionals can supervise laboratory activities and the classroom teacher can provide content instruction and/or operational procedure.

In addition, the media specialist is also often expected to be a technician responsible for the cleaning and maintenance of not only the technologies in the media center but throughout the school. In small districts, technical assistance may be provided by the district computer department or through an external contractor or the technical division of the company from whom the technology was purchased. Larger districts may have a technical support staff that travels from school to school. Rarely does any individual school have enough professional or paraprofessional personnel to cover all responsibilities adequately.

Furthermore, the school library media specialist is expected to serve as technology consultant, advising teachers on hardware and software to serve their instructional needs.

The ALA/AECT guidelines recommend a division of responsibilities, but financial considerations are often used as the final determining factor in making personnel decisions. It becomes the school library media specialist's task to prioritize his responsibilities. Too often the time-consuming tasks of introducing and maintaining new technologies overshadows other responsibilities.

DOE NA   9, 54

3.5.2 Coordinate development of short-range and long-range technology plans.

Development of viable technology plans has been a concern at both the local, district, and state levels. In Florida there are no state guidelines. Most districts have been developing their own plans which will eventually give direction to the formation of state guidelines. Initially, technology plans involved determining the number of pieces of hardware to buy, the installation cost and procedures, and the physical maintenance system. How they would be used for instruction or information gathering was seldom addressed. Only recently has the educational soundness of planning before hardware purchase become a universal concern.

Long-range plans may evolve from district plans for school-to-school connectivity and resource sharing plans as well as from goals that match the local school goals (4.1.4). Preferably, these goals would be included in the School Improvement Plan, and often it is the library media specialist who chairs the technology committee. The 3-5 year plan should address the learning objectives and the technology needed to meet those objectives. It should also project the cost of hardware, software, phone time charges, peripherals, etc. Finally, it should prioritize the goals.

The short-range plan should address one or more priorities and the following related factors:
1. Immediate cost and funding sources.
2. Implementation. What type of hardware, software, and peripherals should be purchased to meet the goals? Are there networking considerations - cabling, electrical outlets, surge protection? Are there concerns about the use of certain technologies - multi-user contracts, dedicated phone lines, monitoring student access to Internet sites?
3. Flexibility. Does the technology have durability and potential future use? Is it upgradable or does it have possible use elsewhere if new or upgraded technology becomes available? Can the goals be adjusted easily as needs change?

DOE NA   9, 52

3.5.3 Participate in workshops and technology conferences on local, district, and state levels.

Attending workshops and conferences is part of the library media specialist's continuing education.

National and state organizations conduct annual conventions (ALA, FAME) and in recent years the Florida Department of Educational and AECT have co-sponsored FETC (Florida Educational Technology Conference). Some districts also conduct local conferences on in-service days. These conferences offer two major benefits:
1. Workshops in innovations in the field and the use of emerging technologies are conducted by experts.
2. Vendors from media and equipment companies display the latest in their product lines.

DOE NA

SKILL 3.6 Recognize role in curriculum planning.

3.6.1 Identify basic methods for instructional planning.

Instructional planning for the school library media specialist is the process of effectively integrating library skills instruction into the curriculum (3.3.1).

Methods of instructional planning:
1. Identify content. Teachers create a list of instructional objectives for specific classes. Library media specialists, using state and local scope and sequence, prepare a list of objectives for teaching information skills.
2. Specify learning objectives. Teachers and library media specialists working together should merge the list of objectives.
3. Examine available resources.
4. Determine instructional factors:
   a. Learner styles.
   b. Teaching techniques and teacher and library media specialist division of responsibilities in the lesson implementation.
   c. Student groupings. Consider abilities, special needs, etc.

5. Pretest.
6. Determine activities to meet objectives.
7. Select specific resources and support agencies.
8. Implement the unit.
9. Evaluate.
10. Revise the objectives and/or activities.

DOE 8.1   24, 30, 35, 41, 47, 49

3.6.2 Identify methods for recognizing curriculum changes.

Since the 1983 publication of *A Nation at Risk*, the curriculum of America's schools has been the subject of much scrutiny. The back-to-basics movement of the 1980's resulted in Florida legislation, which made provisions for the design of a state-wide uniform curriculum. Academic criteria and student minimum performance standards were provided for each course of study. This curriculum facilitated testing students in 4th, 8th, and 11th grades to determine mastery of basic skills and mandated passage of skills on the State Assessment Test (11th) in order to receive a high school diploma. Modifications in the plan over the past decade include adding a writing test in 10th grade, raising the level of minimum standards, allowing greater flexibility in adding electives, and conducting an assessment test in 10th grade to allow for greater preparation for the High School Competency Test given in the 11th grade.

Recognizing curriculum changes requires
1. Analysis of current literature and national or state legislation and guidelines.
2. Study of the existing school and district curriculum and its reflection on current standards and future trends.
3. Consultation with local and district curriculum planners and participation in workshops or programs that address curriculum change.

DOE 8.2   37, 41, 47, 50

3.6.3 Identify resources that present information on educational trends.

Periodicals in the fields of library/information sciences and technology are excellent sources of education trends: *Florida Media Quarterly, Media and Methods, Multi-Media Schools, New Media, Florida Technology in Education Quarterly, School Library Media Quarterly,* and *School Library Journal.*

The *School Library Media Annual,* published since 1983, includes a section on "Trends and Forecasts" in each edition.

State and national conferences include in their workshop structure many programs in educational trends, curriculum change, and innovative ways to use new technologies.

DOE 8.3   41, 47

3.6.4 Understand school library media specialist's role on the curriculum team.

School library media specialist's should be more involved in curriculum planning than current research indicates, both on school and district curriculum teams. Sometimes principals must be coaxed into including school library media professionals in curriculum planning because they occasionally forget that media professionals are technically teaching professionals. The school library media specialist must volunteer to participate and hope that the administration places a value on the contribution she has to offer.

As a team member, the school library media specialist contributes by
1. Advising of current trends and studies in curriculum design.
2. Advising the school staff on the use of media and instructional techniques to meet learning objectives.
3. Ensuring that a systematic approach to information skills instruction will be included in curriculum plans.
4. Recommending media and technologies appropriate to particular subject matter and activities.

DOE 8.4   7, 23, 37, 41, 47, 50

SKILL 3.7 Recognize leadership role in school community.

3.7.1 Identify approaches to promoting collaboration between the library media program staff and other school staff, students, and community groups.

The school library media specialist must establish rapport with all groups in the school community. To promote this collaboration, she should involve representatives from these groups in the development, implementation, and evaluation of the school library media program.
1. Establish a library media advisory committee (4.1.7).
2. Solicit expert advice of teachers on selecting materials for the collection and weeding.
3. Promote the program (5.2) and solicit suggestions for improvement.
4. Establish a reciprocal working relationship with the school principal and/or supervisor of media.
5. Conduct workshops or lessons on using the media center as a resource center.

DOE 20.1   18, 35, 41, 47, 48

3.7.2 Identify leadership techniques that help define the school library media specialist's involvement in the total school program.

A good leader should be able to work and inspire others to work in a team environment where the input of team members at all levels is encouraged and appreciated.

To accomplish this goal, she should
1. Exhibit the desire to achieve the goals of an efficient library media program.
2. Show appreciation for the contributions of library media staff and supervise them in a democratic style.
3. Delegate tasks to responsible staff members.
4. Engage in continuing education.
5. Maintain active membership in professional organizations.
6. Show respect and concern for colleagues and superiors.

DOE 20.2   18, 35, 40, 41, 47, 48

COMPETENCY 4.0 KNOWLEDGE OF AREAS REQUIRED FOR OPERATION OF SCHOOL LIBRARY MEDIA CENTER.

SKILL 4.1 Exhibit knowledge of procedures for establishing, maintaining, and evaluating a successful school library media program.

4.1.1 Identify historical, societal, and technological changes that impact school library media programs.

Until the passage of the Elementary and Secondary Education Act in 1965, which encouraged the evolution of school libraries into library media centers, school libraries were repositories of print material, mainly reference books and fiction. School librarians, rarely having a support staff, circulated and processed materials, supervised student behavior in the library, maintained the collection, and distributed limited equipment. The explosion of information and the retrieval systems for accessing that information has revolutionized the role of the school library media specialist (3.0) and the program she oversees (1.2). Studies in child development by Jean Piaget, Erik Erikson and Lawrence Kohlberg had begun to affect collection development in post-World War II America. Learning style theories from Abraham Maslow's hierarchy to Howard Gardner's seven intelligences have modified classroom teaching.

As libraries began to evolve into full service media centers and school media specialists became instructional consultants to teachers, all aspects of program development were influenced by the need to know these factors that influence children's learning. The ability to assess the needs of student users of a particular media center's services and resources becomes a collaborative effort with classroom teachers who have daily contact with their students; thus, the move to cooperative planning and cooperative learning in the 1990's.

In the 1980's legislative actions at the national and state level (1.1), government concern for widespread literacy, and document findings such as those in *A Nation at Risk* have all reinforced that instruction must be improved in all areas. As a result of private publications, such as James Naisbitt's

Megatrends and *Megatrends 2000* and research by the staff of *School Library Media Quarterly*, the issue of providing more than mere access to the wealth of information affects libraries in the public and private sector. Ultimately, the school library media specialist becomes the agent through which the most aggressive change will occur.

In 1983, Dr. Shirley Aaron, a professor of library science at Florida State University, and Pat Scales, a school library media specialist at Greenville Middle School in South Carolina, undertook a significant project - to produce an annual report. Each volume has sections of articles on issues of current interest, legislation, professional organizations' reports, trends, and forecasts. By 1988, Jane B. Smith, school library media consultant to the Alabama Department of Education, assumed the role of managing editor. Author of several books herself, Ms. Smith has become one of the experts in school library media. Dr. Phyllis Van Orden, also an FSU professor in the Division of Library and Information Management, has authored a major book on collection development.

In 1988, *Information Power* was published under the supervision of AASL president, Karen Whitney, and AECT president, Elaine Didier. In the same year *Taxonomies of the School Library Media Program* by David Loertscher, senior acquisitions editor for Libraries Unlimited, appeared. In fact, there is now a considerable body of excellent reference material on school library media.

Technology has both created the engines of access and contributed to the volume of available information. In addition to learning the types of equipment and their functions and demonstrating their use to teachers and students, the school library media specialist must also locate or design lessons that will teach the 'search and sift' techniques that help them find the appropriate information for a given need. Critical evaluation of the reading and applying the new information to previous knowledge are skills that must be accomplished.

Many school library media specialists have accepted the title without making the adaptation. They feel overloaded by the magnitude of the job description. Oftentimes, districts approach technology enhancement by putting the hardware before the program. Just getting computers, CD players, laser disk players, modems, satellite receivers and so many others in the schools achieves nothing in regard to benefit to the learners, especially if the equipment gathers dust. Program development is often an afterthought, from necessity.

In Florida, the state legislature funded millions for technology block grants at the same time that it failed to increase funds for personnel. When instructional staff must be cut, library media specialists are just as vulnerable as art and music teachers, especially in the elementary schools. The 1990's have been a trying time for media professionals. Fortunately, a strong state professional organization and the determination of the DOE Division of School Media Services staff, under Sandra Ulm, have given the school library media specialist hope and help in recognizing, confronting and coping with the change.

Societal changes have had profound effects on schools. Ethnic diversity, non-traditional families, poverty, and population mobility have created social and cultural problems that did not exist thirty years ago. Furthermore, children raised in this ever-shifting social fabric must be prepared with skills that will enable them to become productive, literate adults. Library media centers are charged with the responsibility of motivating interest in reading as well as promoting acquisition of skills, of providing reading that will not only inform but help children learn how to cope with and enjoy life.

Issues regarding censorship and intellectual access to information increase as the volume of all types of information sources increase. Media professionals must learn how to handle challenges to the material in and accessible from their media centers, and they must guard their patrons' right to free access. Interpreting fair use and other copyright issues requires constant monitoring of court cases and changes in the law (2.3,2.6). The impact of all of these issues has and will continue to affect school library media programs.

DOE 23.1, 23.2, 23.3   1, 17, 41, 45

4.1.2 Identify factors influencing the mission of the school library media program.

The mission of any organization, business, or educational institution should evolve from the needs and expectations of its customers. In the case of the school library media center, its mission must parallel the school's mission and attend to the users' needs for resources and services.

The school library media program should examine school and student characteristics.

School:
1. The mission of the school library media center should reflect and be in harmony with the stated school mission.
2. The program's mission should reflect the curricular direction of the school: academic, vocational, compensatory.
3. The mission should reflect the willingness of the administration and faculty to support the program.

Student:
1. The mission is influenced by pupil demographics: age, achievement and ability levels, reading levels, and learning styles.
2. The mission may indicate the students' interest in self-directed learning and exploratory reading.
3. The mission reflects support from parents and community groups.

DOE 9.1   1, 40, 48

4.1.3 Distinguish a goal from an objective.

A goal is a broad statement of an intended outcome, that gives direction to the program and projects a long-range priority.

An objective is a specific statement of a measurable result that will occur by a particular time, i.e. it must specify the conditions and criteria to be met effectively.

In this Olympic year an appropriate example might be

Goal: To win an Olympic Medal.
Objectives:
1. To increase my speed by .05 seconds per meter by June 30.
2. To double my practice time during the two weeks before the competition begins.
3. To lose 3 lbs. before my weigh-in.

Translated as goals and objectives for library media centers.

Goal: To develop a collection more suited to the academic demands of the curriculum .
Objectives:
1. To increase non-fiction collection by 10% in the next school year.
2. To ensure readability levels suited to gifted students for 5% of new selections.

Goal: To provide telecommunications services within three years.
Objectives:
1. To design a model for instructional use in 1996.
2. To plan for equipment and facilities needs in 1997.
3. To implement the model with a control group in 1998.

DOE 9.2   1, 40, 49

4.1.4 Identify the elements of both short-range and long-range plans for the school library media center.

A goal is a long-range plan. An objective is a short-range plan. Therefore, when planning a school library media program based on an assessment of school and student characteristics, the program planning team should factor in these elements.

A long-range plan should
1. Extend from 3-5 years.
2. Incorporate the goals of the other departments (grade levels or content teams) in the school.
3. Be stated in terms that are non-limiting. The goal should be an achievable aim, not a pipe dream.

A short-range plan should be one part of a longer range plan that is
1. Accomplishable in one year or less.
2. Linked meaningfully in a logical progression to the expressed goal.
3. Flexible, as most objectives must be processed through affected groups before finalization.

DOE 9.3, 9.4   40, 49

4.1.5 Identify components and strategies for evaluating a school library media center program.

Evaluation requires standards, the conditions that should exist if the program is to be judged successful. Some of these standards may already be determined by national or state guidelines that districts administrators have agreed to maintain. Sometimes, a district operates without a program to guide school library media centers. In that case each school must be responsible not only for setting its own criteria but also for inspiring some district planning.

If a school seeks or wishes to maintain accreditation with the Southern Association of Colleges and Schools, using that organization's recommendations is an excellent way to set program goals and objectives. Because SAC requires every accredited school to conduct an intensive ten year reevaluation and five year interim reviews, the library media center program planners may wish to coordinate their own study with the SAC's reviews. *Florida Information Skills K-12* offers qualitative standards for the teaching of skills that can be used in the evaluation process.

Evaluation criteria may be
1. Diagnostic. These are standards based on conditions existing in programs that have already been judged excellent.
2. Projective. These standards are guidelines for conditions as they ought to be ideally.
3. Quantitative. These standards require numerical measurement.

4. Qualitative. These standards are designed to express essentially the measured criteria as quantitative without exact numerical amounts.

Most school library media programs evaluations have been diagnostic or qualitative. Diagnostic prescriptions alone make no allowances for specific conditions in given schools and are often interpreted too liberally; qualitative prescriptions alone are difficult to measure or sustain. Projective standards are usually broad national guidelines which serve best as long-range goals. Preferably, a program evaluation, utilizing a combination of quantitative and qualitative standards, produces results that can lead to modified objectives.

Statistics to substantiate quantitative standards can be derived from
1. Usage statistics from automated circulation systems. These indicate frequency of materials use.
2. Inventory figures. Resource turnover, loss and damage, and missing materials statistics indicate extent of use. Total materials count can substantiate materials per student criteria.
3. Individual circulation logs. Such logs indicate the frequency of patron use of library materials and the types of materials used.
4. Class scheduling log. Depending on the amount of data acquired when a visit is scheduled, several facts can be determined: proportion of staff and student body using materials and services; the frequency of use of specific resources or services; the age levels of users; specific subgroups being served; and subject matter preferences.

Evidence of meeting qualitative standards can be derived from
1. Lesson plans. Careful planning will reveal the frequency of use of resources and specific classroom objectives planned cooperatively with faculty. The plan should also specify the effectiveness with which the students achieved the lesson objectives.
2. Personnel evaluations. Most districts have formative and/or summative evaluations for the professional/para-professional/non-professional staff. Student aides should receive educational credit for their services hours.

Completion of specific skills and termination grades can provide both quantitative and qualitative data.

3. Surveys. A systematic written evaluation should be conducted annually to obtain input from students, teachers, and parents on the success of program objectives.

4. Conferences / Library Advisory Committee meetings. Faculty members' and students' comments can provide qualitative assessment of the value of the materials and services provided.

5. Criterion-referenced or teacher made tests. These assessments can be used to evaluate student effectiveness in acquiring information skills or content area skills.

DOE 10.1   1, 14, 37, 40, 42

4.1.6 Identify participants and their roles in the library media program evaluation process.

Parents, administrators, teachers and students as well as the school library media specialist should be involved in the evaluation process.

Parents should be given an opportunity to react to qualitative standards. In Florida a school improvement survey required every year should have specific items regarding library media.

Administrators' major roles in program evaluation come in the form of conducting personnel evaluations and participation on the library media advisory committee.

Teachers and students can be involved in both formal (an annual survey instrument for the faculty and student body at large) and informal assessments (class discussions and one-on-one interviews.)

The library media advisory committee with representatives from all of these groups should be instrumental in developing assessment instruments, tabulating results, and modifying objectives based on those results.

DOE 10.2   1, 14, 37, 40, 50

4.1.7 Identify role of school library advisory committee.

There are several justifications for a school library media advisory committee. First, all groups affected by the library media program are given an opportunity to provide input during the planning, implementation, and evaluation process. Second, a cooperative plan ensures that all participants accept and promote the program. Third, though slower in completion, a committee-directed plan alleviates having the media specialist shoulder decision-making alone.

No specific guidelines exist for the organization of a library media advisory committee. However, representation from administration, faculty, student body, and parents is essential. The number of participants is affected by student body size and the extent of parent involvement. In elementary schools with active PTA's there may be as many parents as teachers. In secondary schools, where parents take a less active role in their children's education, the committee may struggle to find one parent. Students may be nominated by the faculty, may volunteer, or may be members of a student government subcommittee. Each grade level or content area should have teacher representation, and the principal or her administrative designee should serve.

The role of leader usually falls to the media specialist, though an elected adult chairperson who is not a media specialist is preferable. It is too easy in some schools for the media specialist to do all the work, while the committee merely rubber stamps his decisions and actions.

Some of the activities performed by a library media advisory committee fall into the following four areas.

1. Collection development.
    - making decisions about the purchase of audio-visual equipment and technology hardware and software.
    - assisting with collection weeding.
    - reviewing challenged material.
2. Program planning.
    - reviewing policies and procedures.
    - setting priorities.
    - allocating the budget.

3. Operation (volunteering).
   - teaching information skills.
   - raising funds, especially through book fairs.
   - producing promotional materials (bulletin boards, newsletters, manuals).
4. Evaluation
   - preparing and tabulating results of needs assessment surveys.

Conveniently scheduled meetings should be held regularly, with a specific agenda and minutes. Problem solving activities with specific, attainable goals should be followed by implementation of the solution. Reports of meetings should be communicated to students, teachers, and parent groups.

DOE 9.5   1, 41

4.1.8 Specify uses of program evaluation results.
The purposes of evaluation are to determine if all aspects of planning and implementation have been successfully accomplished. If evaluation shows unsuccessful outcomes, then the program must be modified. Successful outcomes can be used to confirm program objectives and to promote the media center programs.

Some strategies for the use of program evaluation include
1. To produce an annual report to be included in the school's annual report to parents or other publications for circulation in the community.
2. To review and modify long-range goals and plan immediate changes in short-range goals.
3. To lobby for budgetary or personnel support.
4. To solicit assistance from faculty and administration in making curricular or instructional changes to maximize use of media center materials, equipment, and services.
5. To plan greater involvement of students in academic and personal use of media center materials and services.

DOE 10.4   35, 47

SKILL 4.2 Exhibit knowledge of developing policies and procedures for school media center operation.

4.2.1 Distinguish a policy from a procedure.

A policy is the written statement of principle in which the policy-making agency guarantees a management practice or course of action that is expedient and consistent. A procedure is the course of action taken to execute the policy. In government, legislation is policy and law enforcement is procedure.

Educational policy makers include the Congress and state legislatures, state and local school boards, national library media organizations, and school library media program managers. Policies adopted at the local level must support district school board policies and state laws.

Regulations concerning certification, state budget allocations, and standards for selecting and approving state-adopted instructional materials are developed at the state level.

Matters such as collection development and responding to challenges of materials are usually set at district level.

Local issues such as hours of operation, circulation of materials and equipment, and personnel supervision are set by the appropriate school policy makers for library media. Procedures for administering district and state policies are usually determined by usual practice or local precedence.

Procedures for specific administration tasks such as determining budget categories, expending funds, maintaining collection size and so many others should be clearly stated in a school library media procedures manual.

DOE 13.1   18, 40, 48

4.2.2 Identify district policies affecting school media centers.

There are two basic sources for district policies, school board rules (4.2.1) and the procedures manual from district media services offices. Information provided in these documents should be reviewed before any school level planning is done.

It is also necessary to know which policies and procedures are the responsibility of the district and which ones are the responsibility of the school. For example, school boards are charged with the responsibility to set propriety standards for instructional material selection (1.1). However, school boards do not select the texts or library books for individual schools. Procedures for implementing propriety standards are determined at each school site based on the needs of its students.

School boards may set policy for a challenge and identify a procedure for its sequential investigation. The school library media specialist as a defender of intellectual freedom and a trained educator should have the latitude to recommend and purchase quality materials. She should also be prepared to substantiate those purchases in terms of readability, social appropriateness, and artistic quality.

School districts are bound by law to maintain a properly certified staff, but it is the obligation of the employee to learn what and where professional development activities are available, to take six course credits within the five-year period, and to submit proof of same to the certification officer prior to the June 30 deadline in the renewal year.

Operational procedures change from district-to-district. Some counties have centralized reprographics facilities; therefore, district policies are set for reproduction of materials that comply with copyright laws and district procedures for formatting, according to the type of equipment used, are spelled out in a printed manual which should be available at all school sites.

Some counties have centralized materials processing so that classification and cataloging procedures are administered at the county level.

DOE 13.2   41, 48

4.2.3 Identify the participants in the process of formulating policies and procedures.

As indicated in 4.1.7, it is always preferable to develop local policies and procedures with the aid of a library advisory committee.

Participants	Role
Administrator	clarifies school vision and goals.
Media specialist	identifies factors such as time, personnel, resources, and budget that affect school goals.
Teacher	identifies media center resources and services that correlate with instruction.
Student	identifies materials and activities that fulfill learning needs.
Parents (Optional)	identify avenues of communication with parents and community.

Once the advisory committee has formulated acceptable policies and procedures, the district director and/or directors of elementary and secondary instruction should review and provide input before adoption.

DOE 13.3   37, 41

4.2.4 Specify techniques for advertising policies and procedures to the school community.

The most efficient method of communicating policies and procedures to the faculty is the library media procedures manual. This manual should first present the mission and long-range objectives and then the specific policies designed to meet these objectives. Specific procedures for using the resources and services should include scheduling of the facility, circulation of both materials and equipment, requests for consultation or instruction, and requests for production of media.

Communicating policies to students is best facilitated by a structured orientation program and frequent visits to the media center to practice applying those procedures. In schools with closed circuit television, a live or taped program concerning library media use can be very successful.

DOE 13.4, 13.5   1, 18

SKILL 4.3 Exhibit knowledge of sound budget administration skills.

4.3.1 Identify methods of correlating budget issues with program goals and objectives.

In preparation for constructing the budget for the school library media center, the school media professionals need to consider
1. The standards set by state departments of education, local school boards, and regional accreditation associations. Changes in standards sometimes necessitate changes in local budget planning.
2. The sources of funds that support the media center program (4.3.2).
3. The prioritized list of program goals and the cost of meeting these goals.

Determining the relationship between program goals and funding involve the study of
1. Past inventories and projections of future needs.
2. Quantitative and qualitative collection standards at all levels.
3. School and district curriculum plans.
4. Community needs.
5. Fiscal deadlines.

AASL/AECT provides guidelines for four factors in calculating the budget for the print and non-print collection: variation in student population, attrition by weeding, attrition by date, and attrition by loss. A formula for an estimated budget is then calculated based on points established for each of these factors. The estimation for replacement is figured on a base number of collection items required regardless of school size.

The minimum collection standard is determined by the state or regional accreditation requirements.

Another method of estimating a budget for the print collection is based on the types of materials needed: replacement books, periodicals, books for growth and expansion, and reference books. It is recommended that 5% of the total books in the print collection be used in the formula.
Thus, the formula is
   5% x number of books x average cost of book = replacement cost.

For periodicals, multiply the number of periodicals by the average subscription price.

Use the following figures to calculate book collection expansion: at 90% fulfillment of basic requirement, add 3%-5%; at 75%-90% fulfillment, use 10%-15%; and at less than 75%, use 15%-25%. For reference books, multiply the number of sets times the average set price.

In a hypothetical school of 1000-1500 students, SAC recommends a base collection of 9200 volumes plus 5 volumes per student in excess of 1000 students, i.e. a minimum collection of 10,200 books. If that school has only 75% (7650 or fewer), the expansion formula should be
   15-25% x existing collection x average book price.
If our hypothetical school has 7500 books, the formula might be
   20% x 7500 x $20 = $30,000.
If the school has 75-90% of the recommended 10,200 books, we can meet expansion guidelines by adding 10-15% of the collection.
The formula would then be
   10% x 8160 x $20 = $16,320.
Finally, if the school is at 90-100% of the recommendation, we expand by 3-5% or
   5% x 9690 x $20 = $9690.

The SAC standard for periodicals is no fewer than 10 titles or one for each 25 students whichever is greater; after the print subscriptions equal 30 the remaining requirement may be satisfied with non-print resources. Let's assume that this school has 50 print subscriptions and 2 non-print databases.

If the average print subscription price is $20 annually and the average non-print database is $2000, this school should estimate $5000 for periodicals.

If two sets of reference books at an average price of $1000 are needed, the estimated cost is $2000.

Calculations for audio-visual materials follows the same basic pattern. For our school, let's assume that we have calculated this figure into our print collection estimate.

Equipment estimations are based on multiplying four elements: the current inventory replacement value; replacement of lost, stolen, or damaged items; average age of the equipment; and the inflation rate. If our hypothetical school has a current value of $200,000, the average age of items is 5 years, the average replacement cost is $200, and the inflation rate is 1.3 percent, the equipment estimation would be calculated as follows:

$200,000 x 5 = $1,000,000 x .013 = 13,000 + $200 = $13,200

The total estimated collection budget then equals the sum of estimates. At 90% satisfaction of collection requirement, our total would be

$9690 + $5000 + $2000 + $13,200 = $29,890

In districts in which the school library media center allocation is not calculated on local recommendations but on an across the board per capita figure, the school library media specialist must then work with the administration to secure necessary funds from the school budget. If funds are not categorized at the district level, the school library media specialist must then set a percentage for each category based on the previously discussed factors.

Having considered all factors, the budget process should parallel budget plans to the program goals and objectives. To achieve this correlation the process should follow these steps.

1. Communicate program and budget considerations to administration, faculty, student body and community groups, allowing sufficient time for input from all groups.

2. Work with representatives from all groups to finalize short-range objectives and review long-range goals for use of funds.
3. Build a system of flexible encumbrance and transferal of funds as changes in needs occur.
4. As part of the program promotion, communicate budgetary concerns to all interested parties.

DOE 11.1   18, 35

4.3.2 Identify funding sources that support school library media programs.

Unlike public libraries, school library media centers are not usually the recipients of endowments or private gifts. School library media centers receive money from local and state tax dollars. The major portion of the funds come from district allotments for instructional materials or capital outlay that are regulated by the state. Schools that have accreditation must adhere to regional guidelines that assure that accreditation. The funding formulas specifically used for school library media budgets vary from district to district but basically comply with the following regulations.

State:
1. Local operation. In Florida, school boards have ultimate responsibility for district allocations. School library media centers funds are allocated from the district operating budget. The funds may be administered at the district or school level according to a per capita figure, adequate to meet operation costs and contractual obligations.
2. Regional guidelines. SAC produces an expenditures requirement based on student body size, allowing a school to average expenditures over a three-year period in which averaged expenditures do not fall below the standard.
3. State funds provided by special legislation. Once provided as a matching fund option, most special funds in the current decade have been in the form of block grants. In the 1980's thanks to the lobbying efforts of F.A.M.E., the Florida legislature increased funding for library media programs by the amount allocated in the local budgets (1.1) and provided for increased program acquisitions for the state ITV (Instructional Television) collection. The library matching

fund program has been eliminated. Dollars for library materials are allocated from the general instructional materials fund. In the 1990's the legislature funded SUNLINK in collaboration with the DOE's Media Services division and the University of Central Florida. Technology block grants have provided funds for retrofitting schools to create local area networks, wide-area networks, and telecommunications services.

Federal:
1. Block grants included in federal education acts (4.6.3). Awarded to states or specific districts, these grants are limited in scope and time. They must be applied for on a competitive basis and renewal depends on the recipient's ability to prove that grant objectives have been met.
2. Current federal funds are earmarked for innovative technologies not operating costs.

In addition to official funding sources, there are other forms of assistance from the community that should be reflected in the budget plan. Because this assistance is in the form of service rather than real dollars, estimated values must be determined. Some community assistance includes
1. Partnerships with local businesses. Free wiring from cable television companies, guest speakers, distance learning opportunities, and workshops in new technologies are just a few possible services.
2. Education support groups. The education committee of the local chamber of commerce, a private education economic council, or parent associations may conduct fund-raisers or offer mini-grants.

DOE 11.2   18, 41

SKILL 4.4 Exhibit knowledge of personnel management.

4.4.1 Distinguish professional responsibilities and activities from paraprofessional responsibilities and activities.

Professional responsibilities and activities are those outlined in the performance indicators throughout Competency 4. The school library media specialist has responsibility for developing program goals, collection development, budget management, consultation with teachers in using existing resources or producing new materials, provision for student instruction and staff development, and overseeing the paraprofessional and nonprofessional staffs.

The paraprofessional is a person qualified for a special area of media such as graphics, photography, instructional television, electronics, media production, or computer technology. Often called a technical assistant, this person has training in his specialty and some education training but does not have a bachelor's degree in library or information sciences. He may have an AA or BA/BS degree in his specialty. Some community colleges are now offering certificates in Library Assistantship.

The paraprofessional's responsibilities are in the areas of production, maintenance, and special services to students and teachers. Some of his duties might include
1. Working with teachers in the design and production of media for classroom instruction.
2. Creating promotional materials and preparing special need media (video yearbook, audio or videotape duplication, preparation of materials for faculty meetings and staff development activities).
3. Operating and maintaining production equipment (laminator, Thermofax).
4. Maintaining computers and peripherals.
5. Evaluating media and equipment collection and recommending purchases.
6. Developing ways to use existing and emerging technologies.
7. Assisting teachers and students in locating and using media and equipment.

8. Repairing or making provisions for repair of materials and equipment.
9. Circulating equipment.
10. Maintaining records on circulation, maintenance, and repair of media and equipment.

The non-professional staff assumes responsibility for operational procedures (clerical, secretarial, technical, maintenance) that relieve the school library professional and paraprofessional of routine tasks so they can better perform their responsibilities.

Some specific nonprofessional activities:
1. Conducting accounting and bookkeeping procedures.
2. Unpacking, processing and shelving new materials.
3. Processing correspondences, records, manuals, etc.
4. Circulating materials and equipment.
5. Assisting with materials production.
6. Assisting with maintenance and repair of materials and equipment.
7. Handling accounting procedures.
8. Assisting with inventory.
9. Assisting with services provided by electronic and computer equipment.

DOE 12.1   1, 15, 18, 49

4.4.2 Identify appropriate methods to train, supervise, and evaluate school library media staff.

The diversity of user needs, school enrollments, and school/district support services are some factors that affect staff size. Some of the duties of different levels of staff persons overlap and differ only in the amount of decision-making and accountability.

If the school places a high priority on an efficient library media center program, there should be a minimum of two full-time professionals, one paraprofessional and two nonprofessionals, one to function as an office manager and one as a technical assistant. *Florida School Library Media Programs: A Guide for Excellence* in 1976 recommended minimum staff based on student enrollment. Any school from 500-999 should have two library media specialists and one full-time support person. From 1000-1499, there should be two media specialists and two support persons. Schools with student bodies from 1500-1999 should have three full-time media specialists. However, ALA and NEA standards for School Media Programs recommended two support staff for each specialist in any school with under 2000 enrollment. SAC Standards recommend that in a school with two specialists on staff, two paraprofessionals may be hired in lieu of an additional professional. Unfortunately, when schools are looking to save money, it is generally the support staff which is sacrificed.

When the support staff is reduced, the professional must assume operational duties which detract from his professional responsibilities. Volunteers can help with circulation and supplemental tasks that reflect their unique talents and experiences, but they should never be used as substitutes for paid clerical and technical staff. Student assistants, like volunteers, may be trained to assist the media specialist but should not be given duties that are the responsibilities of paid nonprofessionals. They might assist with production of materials, maintenance of the decoration and physical appearance of the center, instruction in materials location, use of electronic/computer databases, and shelving books and periodicals. It is recommended that student aides be given course credit or certificates of achievement to reward them for their services.

Most untrained support staff will need to be trained on the job.
1. Using the district's job description and evaluation instrument for the particular position, prioritize the skills in order from greatest to least immediacy.
2. Determined the already mastered skills by observing performance.
3. Plan a systematic training of remaining skills to be addressed one at a time.

Supervision of media professionals is the responsibility of an administrator. Supervision of support staff is the responsibility of the head library media specialist (if that position is administrative) or of an administrator with input from the media specialist. Periodic oral evaluations and annual written evaluations using the appropriate instrument should be conducted for each media staff member. These evaluations should result in suggestions for training or personal development.

Studies conducted in recent years show that there is a personnel crisis in Florida's school media centers, especially in elementary schools. In an article in *Florida Media Quarterly*, Yahn and Townsend recommended that as many as three different positions - instructional specialist, technology specialist, and media technician - be added to each school staff in order to properly use the technologies for which Florida's Incentive Block Grants have provided.

DOE 12.2, 12.3   18, 49

SKILL 4.5 Exhibit knowledge of school library media center facilities design.

4.5.1 Identify the elements of physical plant design.
A number of factors must be considered in the design, renovation, and maintenance of an efficient library media center.

1. Flexibility of arrangement ensures that as resources and service needs change the facility can be easily modified to reflect these needs. Traffic flow should provide easy, logical access to all spaces.
2. A realistic assessment of security needs will provide for material detection systems, alarms or locks to protect electronic equipment, and convenient placement of communications devices.
3. Proper placement of electrical outlets, fire extinguishers, smoke detectors, and thermostats ensures safety for users and convenience for the staff.
4. Provision must be made for the physically impaired to have barrier-free access to the center and its resources.
5. All areas requiring supervision should be readily visible from other areas of the center.
6. There should be a carefully planned relationship of spaces used for supporting activities and services.

The specifics of spatial arrangement depend upon the types and quantities of resources and services provided. New school design should place the media center in a central location, easily accessible to all academic areas. Within the center itself the following spatial arrangement factors should be addressed.

1. A large central area for reading, listening, viewing, and computing, which has ready access to materials and equipment. AASL/AECT guidelines recommend that this main seating area be 25% - 75% of the total square footage allocation, depending on program requirements. 40 square feet should be alloted per student user. Within this area or peripheral to it should be smaller areas that provide for independent study or accommodate students with physical impairments. Seating should be adequate to accommodate the number of users during peak hours. SAC guidelines recommend floor space and seating to accommodate 10% of the student body, but the media center should not be expected to seat fewer than 40 or more than 100 students at one time.

2. Areas for small or medium-sized group activities. These areas may be acoustically special spaces adjacent to the central seating area or conference rooms, computer labs, or storytelling space. AASL/AECT recommends 1 - 3 areas or approximately 150 square feet with ample electrical outlets, good lighting and acoustics, and a wall screen.

3. Space to house and display the collection. Materials that can be circulated outside the center should be easily accessible from the main seating area. Index tools should be highly visible and in the immediate proximity to the collections they index. A supervised circulation desk with easy access to non-circulable databases (periodicals, CD-ROM disks, microform, and videotape collections) should be close to the center's main entrance. AASL/AECT ecommends 400 square feet minimum for stacks with an additional 200 foot allowance per 500 additional students.

4. A reference materials area within or adjacent to the central seating area. The recommended area allowance is part of the total allotted for the stacks.

5. Space for a professional collection and work area where the faculty and media professionals can work privately. This area should be approximately 1 square foot per student.

EDUCATIONAL MEDIA SPECIALIST

6. Administrative offices, with areas for resource and equipment processing, materials duplication, and business materials storage. An area no smaller than 200 square feet should be available for offices alone and double that area if in-house processing is done.

7. Equipment storage and circulation area close to administrative offices and with access to outside corridor. Space for maintenance and repair is optional depending on available staff to attend to these duties. This space should be no less than 400 square feet for storage with another 150 square feet if repair facilities are necessary.

8. A media production area with space and equipment for production of audio and videotaping, graphics design, photography, computer programming, and photocopying. (In some secondary schools, a dark room is included. Other schools with commercial photography classes and a full photography lab may seek services through the photography teacher.) This area may be as small as 50 square feet or as large as 700 square feet in a school with 500 students depending on the amount of equipment required to suit media production needs; in a school with 1000 or more students at least 700-900 square feet should be allotted for media production.

9. A television production studio for formal TV production class instruction and preparing special programming. Space for distribution of closed circuit programs and satellite transmissions should also be provided. A 1600 square foot studio (preferably 40' x 40' x 15') should be available whenever television classes are taught or studio videotaping is a program priority. AASL/AECT guidelines allow alternatives: studio space available at district for the use of students or mini-studios/portable videotape units where videotaping is done on a small scale.

10. Recommended, but optional in many schools, is a large multi-purpose room adjacent to the media center for use as a lecture hall or meeting room. AASL/AECT recommends that this room be 700-900 square feet in a school with 500 student school (i.e. classroom size) or 900-1200 square feet in a school with 1000 students. This room should be equipped for making all types of media presentations.

DOE 14.1   1, 7, 15, 18, 20, 32

4.5.2 Identify factors that influence the library media center atmosphere.

Because of the diversity of services provided in a modern school library media center, it is important to foster a user-friendly atmosphere, one in which the patron is not only welcomed as a user of resources but is also involved as a producer of ideas and materials.

The library media program, in considering the academic and personal needs of the user, should provide an atmosphere in which users can attain both basic skills and enrichment goals.

Factors that influence the atmosphere:
1. Proximity to academic classes.
2. Aesthetic appearance.
3. Acoustical ceilings and floor coverings.
4. Adequate temperature control
5. Adequate, non-glare lighting with controls for different types of viewing activities.
6. Comfortable, appropriately sized, and durable furnishings.
7. Diverse, plentiful, and current resources that are attractive to handle as well as easy to use.
8. Courteous, helpful personnel, using supervisory techniques that encourage self-exploration and creativity while protecting the rules of library etiquette.

DOE 14.2   7, 15, 18, 20, 32

SKILL 4.6 Exhibit knowledge of collection development, maintenance, and evaluation.

4.6.1 Identify characteristics of collection development policy.

Each school library media center should develop a policy tailored to the philosophy and objectives of that school's educational program. This policy provides guidelines by which all participants in the selection process can get insight into their responsibilities. The policy statement should reflect the following factors.
1. Compatibility with district, state, regional, and national guidelines (1.2).

2. Adherence to the principles of intellectual freedom and the specifics of copyright law.
3. Recognition of the rights of individuals or groups to challenge policies, procedures, or selected items and the establishment of procedures for dealing fairly with such challenges.
4. Recognition of users needs and interests, including community demographics.

The policy should include the school library media center's mission and the criteria used in the selection process. General criteria for the selection of all media include

1. Authenticity. Media should be accurate, current, and authoritative. Copyright or printing dates are indicators of currency, but examination of content is often necessary to determine the relevance of the subject matter to its intended use. Research into the reputations of contributors and comparison to other materials by the same producer will provide insight into its literary quality.
2. Subject matter appropriateness. Suitability to the school's educational objectives, scope of coverage, treatment and arrangement of content, importance of content to the user, and appropriateness to users' ability levels and learning styles must be considered.
3. Appeal. Consideration of the artistic quality and language appropriateness will help in the selection of media that students will enjoy using. Properly selected materials should stimulate creativity and inspire further learning.

DOE 17.1   18, 37, 41, 48

4.6.2 Identify the elements of a collection development plan and the procedure for implementing the plan.

Elements of a collection development plan:
1. Knowledge of the existing collection or the ability to create a new collection.
2. Knowledge of the external environment (the school and community).
3. Assessment of school programs and user needs.
4. Development of overall policies and procedures.
5. Guidelines for specific selection decisions.

6. Evaluation criteria.
7. Establishment of a process for planning and implementing the collection plan.
8. Establishment of acquisition policies and procedures.
9. Establishment of maintenance program.
10. Establishment of procedures for evaluating the collection.

Procedures for implementing the plan
1. Learn the collection. A library media specialist, new to a school with an existing collection, should use several approaches to becoming familiar with the collection.
   a. Browse the shelves. Note your degree of familiarity with titles. Examine items that are unfamiliar to you. Determine the relationship between the materials on similar subjects in different formats. Include the reference and professional collections in your browse. Consider the accessibility of various media and the ease with which they can be located by users.
   b. Locate the center's procedures manual. Determine explanations for any seeming irregularities in the collection.
   c. Determine if any portions of the collection are housed in areas outside the media center.

   If the library media specialist is required to create a new collection, she should
   a. Consult with the district director about new school collection policies.
   b. Examine the collections of other comparable schools.
   c. Examine companies, like Baker and Taylor's, who establish new collections based on criteria provided by the school.
2. Learn about the community.
   a. Examine the relationship of the media center to the total school program and other information agencies.
   b. Become familiar with the school, cultural, economic and political characteristics of the community and their influence on the schools.
3. Study the school's curriculum and the needs of the users (students and faculty). Examine the proportions of basic skills to enrichment offerings, academic or vocational courses, and requirements and electives. Determine the ability levels and grouping techniques for learners.

Determine instructional objectives of teachers in various content areas or grade levels (3.13).

4. Examine existing policies and procedures for correlation to data acquired in researching the school and community.
5. Examine specific selection procedures to determine if guidelines are best met.
6. Examine evaluation criteria for effectiveness in maintaining an appropriate collection.
7. Examine the process to determine that accurate procedures are in place to meet the criteria.
8. Examine the acquisition plan. Determine the procedure by which materials are ordered, received, paid for and processed.
9. Examine maintenance procedures for repairing or replacing materials and equipment, replacing consumables, and discarding non-repairable items.
10. Examine the policies and procedures for evaluation, then examine the collection itself to determine if policies and procedures are contributing to quality and quantity (4.6.5).

Procedures for maintaining the collection are perhaps the most important in the collection plan. The plan itself must provide efficient, economical procedures for keeping materials and equipment in usable condition.

Maintenance policies for equipment and some policies for materials are determined at the district level (4.6.3). Procedures to satisfy these policies are followed at the building level.

1. Replacement or discard of damaged items based on comparison of repair to replacement cost. Districts usually maintain repair contracts with external contractors for major repairs that cannot be done at the school or district media service center.
2. Equipment inventory and records on repair or disposal. Usage records help with the transfer of usable items from school to school.
3. Book bindery contracts.

Policies and procedures for periodic inspection, preventive maintenance and cleaning, and minor repairs are established

and conducted at the school media center.
1. Print material. Spine and jacket repairs, taping torn pages and replacing processing features.
2. Non-print materials. Cleaning, splicing, repairing cases.
3. Equipment. Cleaning, bulb replacement.
4. Inventory and weeding of print and non-print materials; regular replacement of worn or outdated equipment.
5. Record-keeping on items that have been lost or stolen, damaged by nature or neglect, or transferred/discarded.
6. Security systems operation, procedures for emergency disasters, and safe storage of duplicate records.

DOE 18.5, 18.6   15, 29, 37, 48

4.6.3 Identify the relationship between the school and district collection development policies and plans.

District collection development policies may be general or specific but always address areas of concern to all schools. The policy statement should reflect the philosophy of the district, indicate the legal responsibility of the school board, and the delegation of authority to specific individuals at the district and school level. One statement will usually address all instructional materials, including textbook and library media resources.

Some objectives which might be included in the policy:
1. To provide resources that contain information that supports and enhances the school's curriculum.
2. To provide resources that satisfy user needs, abilities, and learning styles.
3. To provide resources that develop literary appreciation and artistic values.
4. To provide resources that reflect the culture and ethnic diversity of society and the contributions of members of various groups to our country's heritage.
5. To provide materials that enable students to solve problems and make judgments relevant to real life.
6. To provide resources that present opposing views on historical or contemporary issues so that students may learn to think critically and objectively.

District plans may deal with

1. Funding policies.
   a. Allocation. School media centers generally receive a portion of the general operating budget. The total amount is determined by a per student dollar amount and may come directly from the district media accounts or, under school-based management, may be apportioned from school budget categories.
   b. Authorization for purchases. These policies vary depending on who has control of the budget: principal, district or media supervisor, district purchasing agent or any combination of the three. In some districts purchase requests must also be approved by curriculum supervisors.
   c. Supplemental sources. Federal or state block grants, endowments, or district capital outlay funds are allocated on a per capita or special project allotment basis. Responsibility for preparation of grant applications is supervised or conducted at the district level. Some districts also set policy concerning the suitability of private donations of material or property items.
2. Preview of considered materials. Some districts seek total control of previewing.
3. Collection size. Districts will frequently set minimum materials and equipment levels, especially if they aim to meet SAC accreditation standards. SAC standard 5.4.1 specifies a minimum book collection which is approximately 10 volumes per student. Responsibility for start-up collections at new schools are governed by district media.
4. Resource sharing. Some decisions in regards to delivery systems, cooperative funding, software licensing and liability are district determined.
5. Time constraints. All districts require that funds be expended by a specific deadline.
6. District media library policies and procedures. Materials that are either too expensive for school budgets and will be used by more than one school are maintained at the district library.
7. Equipment and materials maintenance and repair policy. Districts maintain repair contracts and set procedures for their use. Annual inventories, especially of equipment, are required and periodic assessment of policies are conducted.

8. Central processing. Available in some districts, this department processes materials for convenience and uniformity.

DOE 17.2   15, 37, 41, 48

4.6.4 Identify selection criteria for media and equipment.

In addition to the general selection criteria (4.6.1), certain other specific criteria must be imposed when selecting media and equipment.

Types of media include
1. Printed or display media (pamphlets, handouts, flannel boards, flip charts etc.).
2. Overhead transparencies.
3. Slides and filmstrips.
4. Audiotape recordings.
5. Videotape recordings.
6. Computer software.
7. CD-ROM and laser disks.

Some or all criteria may be applied to the media formats.
1. Technical quality. Sound quality, picture focus, font size, screen color, physical dimensions - these characteristics must be technically correct and artistically appealing for the information within to be appreciated and absorbed by the learner.
2. Packaging. Non-print media need to be packaged in reusable containers if they are to be circulated and if they are to be protected from wear and tear.
3. Cost. The advantages of one format over another must be studied for the limits of the current budget, the size of the group to be served, the durability of the product in terms of the investment. Some products may be considered for rental rather than purchase.
4. Applicability. The product should be suitable for available equipment to use it with, appropriate to the climate and environment in which it will be used, and potentially usable with individuals as well as small or large groups.

5. Educational value. If possible, evidence that the selected media format has been tested with learners to prove its value to the learning process should be provided with the product advertisement.

Equipment criteria:
1. Balance. The amount of audio-visual materials, the frequency of need for these materials, and the preference of teachers will influence the number of items to purchase. District guidelines may set minimum levels.
2. Condition of existing equipment. Some years the budget may be needed for replacement of worn or damaged pieces. Some new equipment is essential to keep up with new media formats.

Selection tools:
1. Company catalogs.
2. State or district approved lists.
3. Services for free or reduced cost products: ITV, MECC.
4. Preview or observation of products.

DOE 18.1, 18.3   7, 15, 24, 30, 37, 48

4.6.5 Identify evaluation criteria and procedures.

Collection evaluation is necessary to determine responsiveness to the school program and instructional needs, access to materials outside the school, preferred user content and formats, and the efficiency of satisfying the media program.

The criteria for evaluating a collection are the same as those for selection (4.6.1 and 4.6.4). Any or all the following procedures may provide data used to measure a collection's value.
1. Comparison of holdings records to bibliographies or catalogs of recommended titles.
2. Comparison of holdings records to lists of specific content or age/ability level materials.
3. Direct examination of the collection to determine size, scope and depth of the general collection or specific areas of the collection. This method also determines the principal condition of materials.

4. Circulation statistics indicate the popularity and frequency of use of certain segments of the collection. Large holdings of materials that do not circulate indicate a need for a policy change. As user needs change, it is necessary to weed materials that have no further application or that have lost their appeal.

5. User opinions, determined from surveys, interviews, or the nature of research being conducted, indicate changes in collection selection. Direct requests from teachers may also be solicited.

6. Application of standards provided by professional library organizations, state departments of education, and regional accreditation commissions must be considered.

DOE 18.1   7, 18, 36, 48

4.6.6 Apply specific selection criteria to materials under consideration.

The following are two examples of ways in which specific criteria may be applied.

1. A secondary science teacher has made a request for a microbiology book that is more readable for introductory or fundamental biology students. Direct examination of existing books reveals that they are all on an advanced reading level. The media specialist should

a. Search available catalogs and materials lists and consult catalogs of other schools (SUNLINK).

b. Validate the credentials of the producers of these titles.

c. Determine the accuracy of content and the currency of the information. Preview requests for direct examination of copies available from publishers or in other collections is necessary.

d. Determine cost, aesthetic appeal, durability of the product, and potential use by other science students.

e. Solicit comments from teachers and students during the preview process.

f. Present a list of titles and let the requesting teacher make selection(s).

2. A pre-K class is added to an elementary school. The media specialist has the responsibility of securing materials appropriate to the younger users.

She should

a. Determine the learning needs of 3 and 4 year olds. Consult with PK-teachers and media specialists in schools with existing PK collections. Use catalogs and other selection tools to construct a list of possible purchases.

b. Compare cost of materials to product durability and quantity needed. Cloth books. learning kits, and puppets, may have greater initial cost but last longer.

c. Factor in accessibility policies and storage limitations. Products purchased with media funds may be best stored in the PK classroom rather than circulated from the media center.

d. Produce a list of recommended materials for committee review and approval.

DOE 18.4   7, 29, 48

4.6.7 Identify resources that assist with the selection process.

Selection of equipment often depends upon the companies represented on the state bid list or local companies with whom the district contracts. Whenever shopping off the bid list, it is advisable to consult the district purchasing agent who may be able to secure better prices than those quoted in company catalogs.

Company catalogs cite specifications of physical dimensions, power needs, etc. For review of quality and performance use periodicals: *New Media, Technology Review, PC Week, MAC Week, Media and Methods*, and consult with other media professionals.

A number of resources may be used in the selection of print and non-print media.

1. Catalogs from publishers and vendors.
2. Bibliographies in outstanding reference books or text books.
3. Lists provided by library associations
   a. *Selected Films for Young Adults*
   b. *Outstanding Books for the College Bound*
4. Standard catalogs
   a. *Children's Catalog*

   b. *Elementary School Library Collections*
   c. *Senior High School Library Catalog*
5. Lists of award winners: Caldecott and Newbery.
6. Lists of notable materials in books on children's literature (Pillon, Sutherland, etc.) and library media publications like the *School Library Media Annual.*

DOE 18.2   7, 18, 36, 41, 48

4.6.8 Identify the components of circulation procedures.

Circulation policies and procedures should be flexible to allow ready access and secure to protect borrowers' rights of confidentiality.

The components of circulation procedures:
1. Circulation system. Whether manual or automated, this system should
   a. Be simple to use for convenience of staff as well as to save time for borrowers.
   b. Provide for the loan and retrieval of print and non-print materials and equipment.
   c. Facilitate the collection of circulation statistics.
2. Rules governing circulation.
   a. Length of loan period.
   b. Process for handling overdues.
   c. Limitations.
      - Number of items circulable to individual borrower.
      - Overnight loan for special items (vertical file materials, reference books, audio-visual materials or equipment).
      - Reserve collections.
3. Rules governing fines for damages or lost materials.
4. Security provisions.
   a. Theft detection devices on print and non-print media.
   b. Straps or lock-downs on equipment transported by cart.

Automated circulation systems, as they become more affordable, have several advantages.
1. Ease and speed of use. Barcodes and scanning devices speed the process. Data is quickly retrievable and saves storage space for cards and card files.

2. Compatible catalog programs. Information on circulation status, descriptions of material type and format, and call numbers are included.
3. Collection evaluation and usage statistics.

Some disadvantages include
1. Cost of equipment, service contracts, and annual updates.
2. Power interruptions.
3. Confidentiality of user information.

DOE 19.1, 19.2   1, 18, 27

4.6.9 Identify elements of inventory procedures and their importance to the evaluation process.

Inventory is the process of verifying the collection holdings and assessing the collection's physical condition. Its purposes are
1. To indicate lost or missing materials. Identify items for replacement.
2. To reveal strengths and weaknesses in collection. Inventory helps identify areas where numbers of materials do not reflect need.
3. To identify materials needing repair. Periodic preventive maintenance can save major repair or replacement cost.
4. To shape the process of weeding. Outdated and damaged or worn materials would be removed to maintain the integrity of the collection's reputation.

Procedures:
1. Specify when inventory will be conducted. Most schools conduct inventories at the end of the school year. Many districts require inventory statistics be turned into the school or district supervisors before media staff vacations.
2. Determine who will conduct inventory. Personnel availability will determine whether inventory will be conducted by professionals, support staff, or some combination, during school hours or during closed time.
3. Examine each item and match it to the holding records. Pull items for repair.
4. Tabulate results and record on forms required by the school or district.

DOE 19.3   7, 48

SKILL 4.7 Exhibit knowledge of collection organization.

4.7.1 Identify various classification systems and their purposes.

Two classification systems are prevalent in the United States.
1. The Library of Congress System uses a system which has been adopted by many colleges and universities since the 1960's.
2. The Dewey Decimal System is used predominately in schools and public libraries.

The purpose of both systems is to provide universal standards of organizing collections. These systems facilitate location of materials within a collection and enable institutions to share information and materials that are uniformly grouped.

DOE 15.1   2, 18

4.7.2 Identify techniques for maintaining bibliographic integrity.

Bibliographic integrity refers to the accuracy and uniformity with which items are catalogued. Following a standard set of international rules, *Anglo-American Cataloguing Rules*, enables users to locate materials equally well in all libraries that subscribe to these rules. To maintain this integrity, catalogers
1. Recognize an International Standard Bibliographic Description (ISBD) that establishes the order in which bibliographic elements will appear in catalog entries.
2. Note changes that occur after each five years review of ISBD.
3. Agree to catalog all materials using the AACR standards.

DOE 15.4   2

4.7.3 Identify bibliographic field records.

The components of a basic bibliographic record (may be used in LCC or DDC shelflist cards or in OCLC's MARC records for automated systems):
1. Call Number. Includes DDC or LCCN classification number followed by a book identification identifier (numerals or letters).

2. Author Main Entry Heading. Use name by which author is most commonly known even if that name is a pseudonym.
3. Title and Statement of Responsibility Area. Include title, subtitle, or parallel titles and name(s) of authors, editors, illustrators, translators, or groups functioning in authorship capacity.
4. Edition Statement. Provide ordinal number of edition.
5. Material Specific Details. Used with only four materials (computer files, cartographic materials, printed music, and serials in all formats).
6. Publication, Distribution, etc. Area. Include place of publication, name of publisher and copyright date.
7. Physical Description Area. Include the extent of the work (number of pages, volumes, or other units); illustrative matter; size/dimensions; and accompanying materials.
8. Series. Provide title of series and publication information if different from statement of responsibility.
9. Notes. Provide information to clarify any other descriptive components, including audio-visual formats or reading levels.
10. Standard numbers. Provide ISBN, ISSN, or LCC number, price, or other terms of availability.

DOE 15.2   2, 13, 19, 27

4.7.4 Identify various ways of providing bibliographic information.

There are three levels of bibliographic description.
1. Level 1 descriptions are the simplest and most appropriate for small or general collections. Although they satisfy AACR standards, they are not considered full records.
2. Level 2 descriptions are more detailed and are used by medium to large libraries where clients use materials for research. Many libraries, including small media centers, use description format somewhere between Level 1 and Level 2.
3. Level 3 descriptions are full records that require application of every AACR rule. Most major libraries, even the Library of Congress, develop some system just short of full Level 3 cataloging.

OCLC bibliographic records (MARC) use both a short form (Level I enhanced) and a long form (Level 2).

It is necessary for all entries to have standardized subject headings. *Sear's List of Subject Headings* is generally used in Dewey Decimal classification while the Library of Congress has its own subject heading list.

DOE 15.3   2, 19

COMPETENCY 5.0 EXHIBIT KNOWLEDGE OF PROMOTION TECHNIQUES.

SKILL 5.1 Identify methods of determining use of library media materials and services.

The primary way of determining use of library materials and services is to examine circulation records. With automated systems it is possible to generate monthly statistics on the number of items circulated. Dividing by the average number of items a user may check out during that circulation period will provide an idea of the number of users who visited the media center.

In elementary schools where whole classes visit on a regular schedule, usage may be tabulated by multiplying class size by the number of visits. In schools with flexible scheduling, keeping a log of visits and the number of participants in each group might result in a truer figure since users may do in-house research, use computers, create media productions, or otherwise use services that do not involve borrowing materials.

DOE 16.1   18, 48

SKILL 5.2 Identify approaches to promoting support for the library media program.

Establish and nurture an administrative partnership with the principal and district director of media to develop, establish, and fund library program goals. In larger districts that have a district director of media, avenues of support may be clearly defined. In smaller districts, where the media director also handles other administrative duties or where there is no district coordinator, support is based on the lobbying efforts of the school library media specialist. In any case, the principal must be the media center's staunchest ally. Present the annual program goals and implementation procedures to the principal early in the school year for his input and approval. Invite him to participate in faculty inservices and advisory committee meetings. Ask to be included on the school's curriculum planning team.

Exhibit your willingness to assume a leadership role in integrating the library media program into the total school program. Make every attempt to ensure that some phase of the library media program appears in each year's school improvement plan.

Work with the district media director and other school library media specialists to establish and maintain a uniformly excellent district library media program. Continually evaluate the goals and objectives of the school program compared to the district program and matched to the users' needs as identified in annual assessments.

Attend school board meetings. Be aware of all issues affecting the media program, instruction, and the budget. Invite county or area superintendents and school board members to district media meetings to discuss issues and plan improvements. Make yourself and your enthusiasm for the library media program visible.

Read widely in the resources listed in 1.3. A knowledgeable library media specialist is the best human resource in the school. There is perhaps no better promotion for the media center than having students, teachers, and administrators seeking information from the library media center staff.

Attend college courses, inservice training, and professional conferences (3.5.3). Offer to teach night college courses, supervise a library media candidate, offer workshops for school faculty, and make presentations at conferences. But, remember to be selective. Never forsake your ethical responsibility to serve patrons by overextending your commitments.

Keep apprised of state certification requirements for certificate renewal and complete renewal requirements (1.9) in a timely manner.

Systematically assess program needs at least annually. Always have available statistics about media center use (5.1), lesson plans or visitation schedules, and written evaluations of instructional activities. Make presentations to School Improvement Committees, parent support groups, or community agencies. Making thorough, accurate reports indicates a well-managed program and encourages maximum support.

DOE 16.2, 16.3   31, 34, 35, 41

COMPETENCY 6.0 UNDERSTANDING OF CHILDREN'S / ADOLESCENT LITERATURE.

SKILL 6.1 Identify outstanding resources that meet the needs of youth.

In addition to the works of Carlsen, Donelson, Huck, and Sutherland, all of which contain excellent information on children's/adolescent interests and needs, the school library media specialist can rely on lists of titles published in other resources. The *School Library Media Annual* includes Caldecott and Newbery winners and notable materials lists such as

1. Notable Books for Children - Association for Library Service to Children of ALA.
2. Children's Reviewers' Choice - Booklist.
3. Children's Choices - The Children's Book Council.
4. Best Books for Young Adults - Young Adult Services Division of ALA.
5. Young Adult Reviewer's Choice - Booklist.
6. Notable Children's Films - ALSC.
7. Selected Films for Young Adults - YASD.

In Florida a committee of FAME annually selects the Sunshine State Young Reader's Award recipients, printing the winners in the spring or summer issue of *Florida Media Quarterly*. Recent winners include

Grades 3-5

1995-96	*Blackwater Swamp*	Bill Wallace
1994-95	*Knights of the Kitchen Table*	Lon Scieszka
1993-94	*Fudge-A-Mania*	Judy Blume
1992-93	*Fudge*	Charlotte Towner Graeber
	No Bean Sprouts Please	Constance Hiser
	The Doll in the Garden	Mary Downing Hahn

Grades 6-8

1995-96	*Seventh-Grade Weirdo*	Lee Wardlow
1994-95	*Devil's Bridge*	Cynthia DeFelice
1993-94	*Nightmare*	Willo Davis Roberts
1992-93	*Something Upstairs*	Avi
	A Doll in the Garden	Mary Downing Hahn
	The Devil's Arithmetic	Jane Yolen

Lists of Caldecott and Newbery awards can also be found in most general encyclopedias.

Though bookseller John Newbery was the first to publish literature for children on any scale in the second half of 18th century England, the great outpouring of children's literature came 100 years later in the Victorian Age. Novels such as Charles Dickens' *Oliver Twist*, Robert Louis Stevenson's *Treasure Island*, and Rudyard Kipling's *Jungle Book*, though not written for children alone, have become classics in children's literature. These books not only helped them understand the world they lived in but satisfied their sense of adventure.

Many of the most popular books for children in the late 19th and early 20th century were translations of foreign favorites like Andrew Lang's *The Blue Fairy Book* (and its rainbow of successors); Astrid Lingren's *Pippa Longstocking*; Johanna Spyri's *Heidi*; and Jean de Burnhoff's Babar Series. Titles in English such as Beatrix Potter's *Tales*; A.A. Milne's *Winnie the Pooh*; and Kenneth Grahame's *Wind in the Willows* have remained popular into the 1990's. The beauty of many of these books is their universality of appeal.

Children's/adolescent literature of the last 50 years has grown to thousands of new titles per year and many tend to the trendy, the authors and publishers being very aware of the market and the social changes affecting their products. Books are selected for libraries because of their social, psychological, and intellectual value. Collections must also contain materials that recognize cultural and ethnic needs. Because so many popular titles, especially in the young adult area, deal with controversial subjects, school library media specialists are faced with juggling the preferences of their student patrons with the need to provide worthwhile literature and maintain intellectual freedom in the face of increasing censorship. Books such as Robert Cormier's *Chocolate War*, *Return to Chocolate War*, and *Fade* deal with the darker side of teen life. Paul Zindel's *Pigman* and *The Undertaker's Gone Bananas* deal with the stresses in teen life with a touch of humor.

Books of the young child reader teach about his relationships to the world around him and to other people and things in that world. They help him learn how things operate and how to overcome his fears. Like the still popular fairy tales of previous centuries, some of today's popular children's books are fantasies or allegories, such as Robert O'Brien's *Mrs. Frisby and the Rats of NIMH*.

Popular books for preadolescents deal more with establishing relationships with members of the opposite sex (Sweet Valley High series) and learning to cope with their changing bodies, personalities, or life situations as in Judy Blume's *Are You There, God? It's Me, Margaret*. Adolescents are still interested in the fantasy and science fiction genres as well as the popular juvenile fiction. Middle school students still read the Little House on the Prairie series and the mysteries of the Hardy boys and Nancy Drew. Teens value the works of Emily and Charlotte Bronte, Willa Cather, Jack London, William Shakespeare, and Mark Twain as much as those of Piers Anthony, S.E. Hinton, Madeleine L'Engle, Stephen King, and J.R.R. Tolkein because they're fun to read whatever their underlying worth may be.

DOE 7.1, 7.4   10, 12, 17, 26, 36, 45

SKILL 6.2 Identify reputable authors and illustrators.

Well-known writers of children's fiction include Betty Byars, Susan Cooper, Shirley Hughes, Sheila Solomon Klass, Elizabeth Speare, Gary K. Wolf, and Lawrence Yep. Children's poets include Nancy Larrick, Maurice Sendak, and Sol Silverstein.

Fiction writers popular with young adolescents include Judy Blume, Alice Childress, Beverly Cleary, Roald Dahl, Virginia Hamilton, Kathryn Lasky, Lois Lowry, Robin McKinley, Katherine Peterson, Teresa Tomlinson, and Bill Wallace.

Older adolescents enjoy the writers in these genres.
1. Fantasy: Piers Anthony, Ursula LeGuin, Ann McCaffrey
2. Horror: V.C. Anrews, Stephen King
3. Juvenile fiction: Judy Blume, Robert Cormier, Rosa Guy, Virginia Hamilton, S.E. Hinton, M.E. Kerr, Harry Mazer, Norma Fox Mazer, Richard Newton Peck, Cynthia Voight, and Paul Zindel.
4. Science fiction: Isaac Asimov, Ray Bradbury, Arthur C. Clarke, Frank Herbert, Larry Niven, H.G. Wells.

Notable illustrators of children's books include Marcia Brown, Leo and Diane Dillon, Barbara Dooney, Nonny Hogrogian, David Macaulay, Emily Arnold McCully, Allen Say, Maurice Sendak, Chris Van Allsburg, and David Wiesner.

DOE 7.2, 7.3   12, 26, 45

RESOURCES

1. American Association of School Librarians and Association for Educational Communications and Technology. *Information Power: Guidelines for School Library Media Programs.* Chicago: American Library Association and Association for Educational Communications and Technology, 1988.

   A sourcebook for presenting professional guidelines for developing school library media programs for the 1990's and into the twentieth century. It includes chapters on establishing and maintaining a school library media program; defining the role of the school library media professional and paraprofessional personnel; determining the resources, equipment, and facilities necessary to meet the goals; and spelling out leadership responsibilities of district, region, and state. Appendices contain policy statements of different organizations, present research results, and provide budget formulas and minimum standards for facilities spaces.

2. American Library Association, Canadian Library Association, and The Library Association. *Anglo-American Cataloging Rules.* 2nd ed. Chicago: American Library Association, 1988.

   A revised edition which provides rules for including technology changes.

3. American Library Association, Office for Intellectual Freedom Staff. *Intellectual Freedom Manual* . 2nd ed. Chicago: American Library Association, 1983.

   Updated in 1998, this manual presents the statements of rights of various library organizations, provides the ALA Intellectual Freedom statement and its implications for library media programs, discusses laws and court cases, advises on methods to deal with censorship, and presents promotion techniques.

4. Anderson, Pauline H. *Planning School Library Media Facilities.* Hamden, CT: The Shoe String Press, Inc., 1990.

   This extensive work traces the creation of a school library media center from politicking to moving in. Much emphasis is placed on the planning process. Five specific case studies are offered to show how the process works.

5. Baker, Philip D. *The Library Media Center and the School.* Littleton, CO: Libraries Unlimited, 1984.

A thorough discussion of the school library media program in relation to the total school mission and objectives.

6. Bannister, Barbara Farley and Janice B. Carlile. *Elementary School Librarian's Survival Guide.* New York: The Center for Applied Research in Education, 1993.

A great guide for either setting up a new media center or operating an existing one. It deals with the physical management of the media center; successful discipline; reading promotions; special programs; story times, book talks, and library skills; building support with the school community; budgeting; selection procedures; new technologies; inventory and weeding; and avoiding burnout. Full of practical suggestions and reproducibles.

7. Brown, J. W.; R. B. Lewis; and F. F. Harcleroad. *A V Introduction: Technology, Media, and Methods.* 6th ed. New York: McGraw-Hill, 1983.

A good reference book on the use of instructional materials and technology at all educational levels. It provides information on planning instruction, using and producing various media, operating audio-visual equipment, and designing facilities for using media. It also provides information on copyright laws.

8. Buchanan, Jan. *Flexible Access Media Programs.* Littleton, CO: Libraries Unlimited, 1991.

A fine reference tool for understanding and developing approaches to designing flexible access programs for school library media centers. Presents an overview of current research on integrating the teaching of library skills into the curriculum, a whole language approach to teaching reading, and the importance of encouraging critical thinking. The book's greatest value is showing the building level media specialist the techniques for involving the total school community in the planning and implementation of integrated lessons and defining the roles of all the participants involved in the planning, execution and evaluation stages. Emphasis is on the cooperative planning required and on the measurable benefit to the learner.

9. Bucher, Katherine Toth. *Computers & Technology in School Library Media Centers*. Worthington, OH: Linworth Publishing, Inc., 1994.

This 3-ring bound publication offers a thorough discussion of technology's relevance to libraries. It includes as contents (1) working with instructional technology in the 1990's, (2) computer basics, (3) library management with a computer, (4) multimedia CD-ROM, (5) videodisks in the library.

10. Carlsen, G. Robert. *Books and the Teenage Reader.* New York: Harper and Row, 1971.

This ageless work discusses teenage interests and social/personal needs and provides reading lists in different genres, interest areas, classics, etc.

11. Curley, Arthur. "Yes for ALA Goal 2000." *Florida Media Quarterly* 1995: Volume 20, Number 3: 24.

A short article specifying the Goal 2000 theme and the value of its message for school library media programs.

12. Donelson, K. L. and A. P. Nilsen. *Literature for Today's Young Adults.* 3rd ed. Glenview, IL: Scott, Foresman, 1989.

A textbook dealing with print media: the history and trends of young adult literature; genres of special interest; using materials with young adults; and guidelines for evaluating these works. Presents brief statements about works of both recognized merit and potential interest to young adults and sketches of authors known in the field.

13. Downing, Mildred Harlow and David H. Downing. *Introduction to Cataloging and Classification.* 6th ed. Jefferson, NC: McFarland & Company, Inc., 1992.

A basic primer on cataloguing techniques and classification systems.

14. Florida Department of Education, Division of Public Schools, Bureau of Program Support Services, School Library Media Services Section. *Information Skills for Florida Schools K-12*. Tallahassee, FL: Florida Department of Education, 1984.

    A concise scope and sequence for the teaching of library skills. Offers a fold-out chart for readily identifying skills, at their introductory, review, reinforcement, and expansion stages.

15. Florida Department of Education, School Library Media Services Section. *Florida School Library Media Programs: A Guide for Excellence*. Tallahassee, FL: Florida Department of Education, 1976.

    State guidelines, developed from the 1975 AASL-AECT *Media Programs: District and School*, establishing criteria for local, district, and state media services. It details for school level media personnel the program responsibilities, operational procedures, personnel duties, resource development, and facilities.

16. Florida Division of Statutory Revision of the Joint Legislative Management Committee. *Official Florida Statutes, 1993*. Tallahassee, FL: State of Florida.

    Biennial set of complete laws governing the state, published in odd numbered years. Supplements printed in even numbered years.

17. Gillespie, J. T. (Ed.) *Best Books for Junior High Readers*. New Providence, NJ: Bowker, 1991.

    A reference guide to selecting titles for junior high (upper middle school) readers. Presents examples of literature within certain genres, discusses themes appropriate to middle grade readers based on personal, social, and academic needs.

18. Gillespie, J. T. and D. L. Spirt. *Administering the School Library Media Center*. New York: Bowker, 1983.

    A guide to practical considerations in operating a school library media center. Chapters on acquisition, organization, and management, with chapters on new technologies. Presents example of a policies and procedures manual. Revised in 1993.

19. Hagler, Ronald. *The Bibliographic Record and Information Technology.* 2nd ed. Chicago, IL: American Library Association, 1991.

   A serious, detailed study of cataloging, bibliographic standards and controls using MARC record format.

20. Hannigan, J. A. and Glenn Estes. *Media Center Facilities Design.* Chicago, IL: American Library Association, 1978.

   Expanding on the ALA discussion of facilities design in *Information Power* these authors have presented methods and models for media facilities for all school levels, discussing factors for planning, design, and construction even offering architectural renderings.

21. Hart, Thomas. *Behavior Management in the School Library Media Center.* Chicago, IL: American Library Association, 1985.

   A serious work on the positive educational strategies for managing student behavior in the use the resources and services of the school library media center.

22. Haycock, Ken. "Research in Teacher-Librarianship and the Institutionalization of Change." *School Library Media Quarterly* (Summer 1995): 227-233.

   This paper contends that there is ample research to prove the relationship between student achievement and the instructional role of library media specialist. Mr. Haycock offers this evidence and a 92 item annotation to point out the strong statistical support that can be used to promote programs.

23. ——. *The School Library Program in the Curriculum.* Englewood CO: Libraries Unlimited, Inc., 1990.

   This collection of essays/opinion papers by Haycock and others deals with the media center in the context of the total school, the role of the teacher librarian, program planning and development, integrating information skills across the curriculum, secondary school applications, and issues and concerns.

24. Heinrich, R.; M. Molenda; and J. D. Russell. *Instructional Media and the New Technologies of Instruction.* 2nd ed. New York: Macmillan, 1985.

A textbook source for planning and use of non-print media. Full of charts, diagrams, and appendices on sources for free and inexpensive materials.

25. Helm, V. M. *What Educators Should Know About Copyright.* Phi Delta Kappa Educational Foundation, 1986.

A brief, but thorough, discussion of copyright law, the court cases that have tested that law, and the implications of the rulings on schools, including library media programs.

26. Huck, C. S.; S. Hepler; and J. Hickman. *Children's Literature in the Elementary School.* 4th ed. New York: Holt, Rhinehart and Winston, 1987.

Both a textbook in child development and the literature designed to meet children's needs, a study of genres, and a presentation of methods for teaching children's literature. Lists of book awards, authors, illustrators, periodicals and publishers .

27. Inter, Sheila S. *Circulation Policy in Academic, Public, and School Libraries.* New York: Greenwood Press, 1987.

This book deals with circulation policies in academic, public, and school libraries. Specific circulation plans from schools around the country offer models.

28. Inter, Sheila S. and Jean Weichs. *Standard Cataloguing for School and Public Libraries.* Englewood, CO: Libraries Unlimited, 1990.

Written for public librarians and school library media specialists, this book explains the principles and standards of cataloging. Though a thorough discussion of AACR rules, descriptions, subject headings, classification systems, etc., the book avoids discussing arcane details that are most likely not encountered by the intended audience.

29. Katz, W. A. *Introduction to Reference Work.* (Vol. 1) Basic Information Sources. 5th ed. New York: McGraw Hill, 1987.

A study of traditional basic reference sources and methods for using these sources to answer reference questions. Includes an overview of the reference process and on-line reference services and their applications.

30. Kemp, J. E. *Planning and Producing Audio-visual Materials.* 4th ed. New York: Harper & Row, 1980.

Practical guide to media production techniques and methods of instruction Summarizes research on the effectiveness of instructional materials and explains the method of developing an instructional program.

31. Kinney, Lisa F. *Lobby for Your Library-Know What Works.* Chicago, IL: American Library Association, 1992.

Chapter 8 deals specifically with lobbying for schools, presenting typical funding sources and offering strategies to be used by key participants in lobbying agencies from local to state.

32. Klasing, Jane P. *Designing and Renovating School Library Media Centers.* Chicago, IL: American Library Association, 1991.

A quick reference for use by school personnel in planning and implementing an efficient facilities design. Sample floor plans and appendices full of bid forms, architectural symbols, and furniture details simplify the process.

33. Lance, Keith Curry. *The Impact of School Library Media Centers on Academic Achievement.* Castle Rock, CO: Willow Research and Publishing, 1993.

Predominantly a research-based discussion of factors of library media programs that have directly influenced the improvement in student grades, standardized scores, and self-directed learning.

34. Laughlin, Mildred Knight and Kathy Howard Latrobe. (Eds.) *Public Relations for School Library Media Centers*. Englewood, CO: Libraries Unlimited, 1990.

Seventeen articles about different facets of promoting the school library media program, including definitions of public relations, the library media specialist's attitude and interpersonal skills, stress and public relations, and specific groups to motivate.

35. Loertscher, D. V. *Taxonomies of the School Library Media Program*. Englewood, CO: Libraries Unlimited, 1988.

One of the most outstanding works on elements of the school library media center program. Outlines the roles of media professionals, students, teachers, and administrators in integrating the library media program into the school curriculum. Models for personnel and program evaluation are included in appendices.

36. Pillon, N. B. *Reaching Young People Through Media*. Littleton, CO: Libraries Unlimited, 1983.

Fifteen articles dealing with such topics as reading interests, materials selection, genres, censorship, youth advocacy, and technology .

37. Prostano, Emanuel T. and Joyce S. Prostano. *The School Library Media Center*. 3rd ed. Littleton, CO: Libraries Unlimited, 1982.

Revised in 1987, this book deals with the library media center program development, administration and evaluation. There are also chapters on curriculum integration, media personnel, facilities and furniture, media and equipment, and the budget.

38. Reichman, Henry. *Censorship and Selection-Issues and Answers for Schools*. Chicago, IL: American Library Association, 1993.

This book addresses the specific problems of intellectual freedom encountered in schools. It discusses issues that are in dispute, selection policies and the law. It also offers possible solutions to complaints.

39. Report from the White House Office of the Press Secretary on the 1991 White House Conference on Library and Information Services. *Florida Media Quarterly* (Spring 1992), 16-17.

   An article summarizing President Bush's comments resulting from the conference in which he pledges executive support for full literacy by the year 2000.

40. Riggs, D. E. *Strategic Planning for Library Managers.* Phoenix, AZ: Oryx Press, 1984.

   A thorough guide for planning for all types of libraries, especially useful in discussing leadership, organization, and evaluation techniques. Especially effective in defining mission statement and distinguishing between goals and objectives.

41. *School Library Media Annual.* Shirley Aaron and Pat Scales (Eds.) [1983-1987 eds.] and Jane Bandy Smith (Ed.) [1988-1990 eds.] Littleton, CO: Libraries Unlimited.

   Each volume contains articles on national and state legislation, professional organizations, government affairs, and publications of note. Individual volumes highlight special issues.

   Volume 1: adolescent development, intellectual freedom, certification, instructional radio and television, software evaluations, networking.

   Volume 2: lobbying, continuing education, declining enrollment, impact of library media programs on student achievement, telecommunications.

   Volume 3: censorship; intellectual freedom committees, copyright concerns, interactive video, microcomputers in schools, ethical considerations.

   Volume 4: professionalizing the media profession; planning effective programs; information skills; facilities design; intellectual freedom, censorship, and copyright; managing on-line services.

   Volume 5: copyright for new technologies; selection policies and procedures; continuing education; leadership skills; advisory committees; promoting information and inquiry skills.

Volume 6: whole language impact on media, censorship, research on library media centers, updates on automation.

Volume 7: measuring services, developing standards, personnel, flexible scheduling, accreditation, state guidelines, implementing *Information Power*, partnership of NCATE and ALA/AASL.

Volume 8: instructional consulting role, principal's role in creating vision for school library media programs, learning styles, designing effective instruction, contributions of technology, information literacy.

42. Smith, Jane Bandy. *Achieving A Curriculum-Based Library Media Center Program-The Middle School Model for Change.* Chicago, IL: American Library Association, 1995.

This book presents information and practical models for integrating information skills into the school curriculum. This is a sequel to Smith's *Library Media Center Programs for Middle Schools.*

43. ——. *Library Media Center Programs for Middle School: A Curriculum-Based Approach.* Chicago, IL: American Library Association, 1989.

This book presents information on planning and evaluating middle school media programs. It offers procedures in library program development as well as ways of correlating library skills with classroom instruction.

44. Stein, Barbara L. and Risa W. Brown. *Running A School Library Media Center-A How-to-do-it Manual for Librarians.* New York: Neal-Schuman Publishers Inc., 1992.

A practical handbook includes chapters on getting started, administration, ordering and processing materials, cataloging, circulation, maintaining the collection, hiring and working with staff, designing and using the facility, and programming the media center.

45. Sutherland, Zena and M. H. Arbuthnot. *Children and Books.* 7th ed. Glenview, IL: Scott Foresman, 1986.

Chapter One of Part One, "Children and Books Today," discusses the history and direction of children's literature, influences on children's literature, child psychology theories and their application to cognitive development. Chapter Two, "Guiding Children's Book Selection," discusses evaluation standards and examines the elements and range of children's literature. Subsequent chapters provide titles and summaries of recommended literature for various age groups.

46. Talav, Rosemary. *Common Sense Copyright.* New York: McFarland, 1986.

   A practical guide to applying copyright laws in school environments, one chapter specifically addressing media centers.

47. Turner, P. M. *Helping Teachers Teach: A School Library Media Specialist's Role.* Littleton, CO: Libraries Unlimited, 1985.

   An exploration of the school library media specialist's role as a curriculum consultant , with specific suggestions for methods to help teachers design and evaluate classroom lessons using media resources. Also provides information on professional collection development, instructional materials selection and evaluation, and in-house workshop design. Revised in 1988 and 1993.

48. Van Orden, Phyllis J. *The Collection Program in Schools.* Englewood, CO: Libraries Unlimited, 1988.

   A textbook for media professionals on collection development. Divided into three parts: *The Setting* issues, procedures, and policies; *Selection of Materials* addresses selection criteria; and *Administrative Concerns* covers acquisition, maintenance, evaluation, and meeting special needs.

49. Walker, H. T. and P. K. Montgomery. *Teaching Library Media Skills. An Instructional Program for Elementary and Middle School Students.* Littleton, CO: Libraries Unlimited, 1983.

   Another good source for using both print and non-print sources to teach library skills. It offers subject related activities for required and elective subjects as well as discussing the aspects of instruction.

50. Wehmeyer, L. B. *The School Librarian as Educator.* 2nd ed. Littleton, CO: Libraries Unlimited, 1984.

   A text which examines the school library media specialist's role as instructor, offering practical suggestions for library skills instruction and including appendices with games and activities appropriate to both elementary and secondary media centers.

51. Winn, Patricia. *Integration of the Secondary School Library Media Center into the Curriculum.* Englewood, CO: Libraries Unlimited, 1991.

This title specifically addresses the role of the media specialist in integrating the media program into the curriculum and some methods to use.

52. Woolls, E. Blanche and David V. Loertscher (Eds.) *The Microcomputer Facility and the School Library Media Specialist.* Chicago, IL: American Library Association, 1986.

This book is a series of essays in four areas: planning the facility, operating the facility, services of the facility, and working with the facility. From district level networks to microcomputers used for circulation, the microcomputer is here presented as a tool to ease the burden of library media management.

53. Wright, Keith. *The Challenge of Technology-Action Strategies for the School Library Media Specialist.* Chicago. IL: American Library Association, 1993.

Mr. Wright wrote this book because of a concern that technology be used appropriately in education. He addresses the challenges that new technologies have created for the media professional, discusses techniques that schools or districts have used to deal with these challenges, and suggests ways that school library media specialists can prioritize their growing responsibilities.

54. Yahn, Christina and Ronald Townsend. "Media Centers: Still the Instructional Hub of Schools." *Florida Media Quarterly* 1995: Volume 20, Number 4: 10-11.

An excellent article on the importance of school media centers as the source of integrated learning. The authors stress that Florida's Technology Incentive Grants have expanded technology to the degree that additional human resources are needed to use new technologies effectively in the schools.

DIRECTIONS: Read each item and select the best response.

1. In what area of a bibliographic record can the name of the author be found?

   A. physical description area.

   B. publication area.

   C. terms of availability area.

   D. title and statement of responsibility area.

2. In the instructional development process, the K-3 library media specialist might assist the teacher by

   A. checking out a classroom set of encyclopedias.

   B. identifying a list of resources to meet various instructional objectives.

   C. assigning the media assistant to work as a teacher's aide in the classroom so that the teacher could do individual or small group instruction.

   D. showing the teacher how to use the library's automated catalog program.

3. According to AASL-AECT guidelines, for each full-time library media specialist, the school should provide

   A. 1/2 time paid assistant, clerk, or technician.

   B. 1 or more full-time paid assistants.

   C. 2 paid assistants.

   D. no recommendation.

4. Contemporary library media design models should consider which of the following an optional need?

   A. flexibility of space to allow for reading, viewing, and listening.

   B. space for large group activities such as district meetings, standardized testing, and lectures.

   C. traffic flow patterns for entrance and exit from the media center as well as easy movement within the center.

   D. adequate and easily rearrangeable storage areas for the variety of media formats and packaging style of modern materials.

5. Which of the following is the least effective way of communicating school library media policies, procedures, and rules to media center patrons?

   A. announcements made in faculty and parent support group meetings.

   B. a published faculty procedures manual.

   C. written guidelines in the student handbook or special media handbill.

   D. a videotape orientation viewed over the school's closed circuit television system.

6. Florida State Law 231.15 identifies a school library media specialist as

   A. a licensed support person.

   B. an instructional employee.

   C. a non-instructional employee.

   D. an administrator /supervisor.

7. According to Florida State Statute 233.34, a district may use up to what percentage of its instructional materials budget for the purchase of instructional materials or library books that are not on the state-adopted materials list?

A. 30   C. 50

B. 40   D. 60

8. According to the AASL-AECT national guidelines, which of the following is NOT one of the three overlapping roles of the school library media specialist?

A. information specialist.

B. equipment technician.

C. teacher.

D. instructional consultant.

9. The award given for the best children's literature (text) is

A. the Caldecott.

B. the Newbery.

C. the Pulitzer.

D. the Booklist.

10. FAME (Florida Association for Media Education) produces a publication titled

A. the *Florida Media Quarterly*.

B. the *Florida Forum*.

C. *New Media*.

D. *School Library Media Quarterly*.

11. Which of the following is an essential concept in AASL-AECT national guidelines?

A. The school library media program should strive to become an autonomous unit, requiring as little need for interlibrary access as possible.

B. The school library media program should provide intellectual, social, cultural, and economic freedom of access to information and ideas.

C. The school library media program should attune itself to the cultural and ethnic demands of its geographical location.

D. The school library media program should measure its effectiveness by the emphasis it places on the using financial resources to increase its access to current technologies.

12. Coordination of the planning and development of K-12 library media programs that serve the students and staff within the schools is primarily the responsibility of

A. the school library media specialist.

B. the district library media director.

C. the state library media director.

D. the national Secretary of Education.

13. Which of the following instructional media would be the most beneficial to a student engaged in self-paced (individualized) learning?

    A. overhead transparencies.

    B. videotapes.

    C. computer-assisted software.

    D. slides.

14. In which learning pattern would an overhead projector with prepared transparencies be most advantageous?

    A. presentation of information of large groups of students.

    B. self-paced (individualized) learning.

    C. small group interaction between students and instructor.

    D. all three patterns equally well.

15. Which periodical contains book reviews of currently published children and young adult books?

    A. *Phi Delta Kappan*

    B. *School Library Journal*

    C. *School Library Media Quarterly*

    D. *American Teacher*

16. When a parent complains about the content of a specific title in a library media collection, the library media specialist's first course of action in responding to the complaint is to

    A. remove the title from the shelf and purge it from both the catalog and the shelf list.

    B. place the book in reserve status for circulation at parent request only.

    C. submit the complaint to a district review committee.

    D. explain the principles of intellectual freedom to the complaining parent.

17. The **development of policies for circulation of materials at a specific school site should involve**

    A. one or more members of the lay community.

    B. one or more student representatives.

    C. the district media coordinator.

    D. a school board member.

18. The most efficient method of assessing which students are users or non-users of the library media center is reviewing

    A. patron circulation records.

    B. needs assessment surveys of students.

    C. monthly circulation statistics.

    D. the accession book for the current year.

19. In a school with one full-time library media assistant (clerk), which of the following are responsibilities of the assistant?

    A. selecting and ordering titles for the print collection.

    B. performing circulation tasks and processing new materials.

    C. inservicing teachers on the integration of media materials into the school curriculum.

    D. planning and implementing programs to involve parents and community.

20. The first step for students designing their own videotape product is

    A. preparing the staging of indoor scenes.

    B. assembling a cast.

    C. creating a storyboard.

    D. calculating a budget.

21. When a secondary school has two full-time library media specialists, their duties may best be divided as follows:

    A. human resource manager and materials/equipment manager.

    B. audio-visual department supervisor and print/reference librarian.

    C. technician and teacher.

    D. media center supervisor and liaison to faculty, administration, and parents.

22. The English I (9th Grade) teacher wants his students to become familiar with the contents of books in the reference area of the school library media center. He asks the library media specialist to recommend an activity to accomplish this goal. Which of the following activities would best achieve the goal?

    A. Assign a research paper on a specific social issues topic.

    B. Require a biography of a famous person.

    C. Design a set of questions covering a variety of topics and initiate a scavenger hunt approach to their location.

    D. Teach students the Dewey Decimal system and have them list several books in each Dewey subcategory.

23. According to Southern Association accreditation standards, a high school library media center should have

    A. 5 books per student.

    B. 7 books per student.

    C. 10 books per student.

    D. 12 books per student.

24. According to SAC standards what percentage of any library's floor space should be devoted to a professional library?

    A. 5%   C. 15%

    B. 10%   D. no minimum required

25. All of the following are authors of young adult fiction EXCEPT

    A. Paul Zindel.

    B. Norma Fox Mazer.

    C. S.E. Hinton.

    D. Maurice Sendak.

26. The Florida DOE's statewide union database is called

    A. QUICKLINK.

    B. DOWNLINK.

    C. SUNLINK.

    D. SCHOOLLINK.

27. Which of the following is the least necessary software application for computers located in the circulation area?

    A. periodical indices.

    B. reference tools.

    C. word processing.

    D. book catalog.

28. A vertical file is one method of providing easy access to

    A. current events articles in local newspapers.

    B. student publications.

    C. archival school records.

    D. back-issue periodicals.

29. The most effective method of initiating closer contacts with and determining the needs of classroom teachers is to

    A. ask to be included on the agenda of periodic faculty meetings.

    B. present afterschool or weekend inservices in opening communication channels.

    C. request permission to be included in grade-level or content-area meetings.

    D. establish a library advisory committee with one representative from each grade level or content area.

30. A student asks for assistance in locating a copy of Oliver Wendell Holmes' poem "Old Ironsides." The library media specialist should direct her to

    A. the card catalog.

    B. the *Oxford Companion to American Literature*.

    C. a contemporary poetry anthology.

    D. *Granger's Index to Poetry*.

31. The most appropriate means of obtaining extra funds for library media programs is

    A. having candy sales.

    B. conducting book fairs.

    C. charging fines.

    D. soliciting donations.

32. The most important consideration in the design of a new school library media center is

   A. the goals of the library media center program.

   B. the location of the facility on the school campus.

   C. state standards for facilities use.

   D. the demands of current technologies.

33. Current studies of fiscal responsibility to schools recommend that federal funds be used for

   A. capital improvement projects.

   B. operating expenses.

   C. innovative instructional activities using technology.

   D. teacher training and inservice programs.

34. When selecting computer information databases for library media center computers, which of the following is the least important consideration?

   A. cost.

   B. format.

   C. user friendliness.

   D. ability levels of users.

35. Since the inception of *Blueprint 2000,* school library media programs can be evaluated and improved by

   A. a study of materials circulation.

   B. reactions from the library media committee.

   C. an independent needs assessment survey.

   D. the school improvement plan.

36. Recognition of children's book authors and illustrators is presented by

   A. the FAME intellectual freedom committee.

   B. the Sunshine State Book awards.

   C. the Pineapple Press.

   D. the DOE division of media services.

37. Which of the following publishers does NOT figure significantly in the production of library media professional materials?

   A. Bowker.

   B. the Center for Applied Research.

   C. Libraries Unlimited.

   D. Rosen.

38. In 1981, one piece of federal legislation included authorizing thirty-three block grants to states, one of which included funding for library media resources and instructional materials. This bill was the Educational Consolidation and Improvement Act better known as

    A. Chapter I.
    B. Chapter II.
    C. Title I.
    D. Title II.

39. In *Information Skills for Florida Schools K-12*, the ability to use the card catalog to locate sources of information first appears as an application skill in grade

    A. 3-4.
    B. 5-6.
    C. 7-8.
    D. 9-12.

40. In *Information Skills ...* the ability to identify the concept of intellectual freedom is introduced as an appreciation skill in grade

    A. 3-4.
    B. 5-6.
    C. 7-8.
    D. 9-12.

41. Which of the following is a library policy, not a procedure?

    A. providing a vehicle for the circulation of audio-visual equipment.

    B. setting guidelines for collection development.

    C. determining the method for introducing an objective into the school improvement plan.

    D. setting categorical limits on operating expenses.

42. Several Skills in *Information Skills ...* are worded exactly the same from K-12 because the students' mastery of the skill depends on performing that skill at ever advancing levels, even beyond graduation. Which of the following is one of those same worded skills?

    A. Examine award-winning materials.

    B. Identify parts of a book.

    C. Use materials without violating copyright laws.

    D. Use appropriate sources to locate information.

43. "Fair Use" policy in videotaping off-air from commercial television requires

    A. show in 5 days, erase by the 20th day.

    B. show in 10 days, erase by the 30th day.

    C. show in 10 days, erase by the 45th day.

    D. no restrictions.

44. Which fiction genre do these authors- Isaac Asimov, Louise Lawrence, and Andre Norton - represent?

    A. adventure.

    B. romance.

    C. science fiction.

    D. fantasy.

45. Licensing has become a popular means of copyright protection in the area of

    A. duplicating books for interlibrary loan.

    B. use of software application on multiple machines.

    C. music copying.

    D. making transparency copies of books or workbooks that are too expensive to purchase.

46. A material's medium having two or more basic media packaged together as a unit is called a kit. Which of the following is, however, not considered a kit?

    A. a videotape with a study guide.

    B. a sound filmstrip with worksheets.

    C. an audiocassette with a book.

    D. a filmstrip with a record.

47. According to staffing recommendations in *Florida School Library Media Programs: A Guide for Excellence*, a school with a student body of 1500-1999 students should have a minimum of how many professional library media specialists?

    A. 1   C. 3

    B. 2   D. 4

48. Collection development principles in *Florida School Media Programs: a Guide for Excellence* recommend that

    A. only materials housed in the media center should be catalogued.

    B. only materials purchased with media center funds should be catalogued.

    C. all school-owned media resources should be catalogued in the media collection.

    D. no purchase of materials already held in the district media catalog.

49. School library media specialists as instructors must be able to construct statements of objectives for instructional purposes. Which of the following is a properly stated objective?

    A. To describe the process necessary to locate books on Third World countries in the reference area.

    B. To demonstrate the use of the library's automated catalog to aid a newcomer in determining whether a particular title is available.

    C. To understand how the Dewey Decimal System works.

    D. To identify ten authors who have contributed to economic, social, or cultural changes in the 20th century.

50. Under the copyright brevity test, an educator may reproduce without written permission

   A. 10% of any prose or poetry work.

   B. 500 words from a 5000 word article.

   C. 240 words of a 2400 word story.

   D. no work over 2500 words.

51. According to *Information Power*, which of the following is NOT a responsibility of the school library media specialist?

   A. maintaining and repairing equipment.

   B. instructing educators and parents in the use of library media resources.

   C. providing efficient retrieval systems for materials and equipment.

   D. planning and implementing the library media center budget.

52. According to AASL/AECT facilities guidelines, how many square feet should be provided per student in the main library seating area?

   A. 16   C. 25

   B. 20   D. 40

53. AASL/AECT budget formulas recommend what percentage of a print collection be replaced annually because of loss, damage, or wear that is beyond repair?

   A. 5%   C. 15%

   B. 10%   D. 20%

54. Which of the following periodicals uses a unified theme approach for each issue?

   A. *Educational Digest*

   B. *School Library Journal*

   C. *Phi Delta Kappan*

   D. *American Teacher*

55. Which of the following has made the greatest impact on school library media centers in the last decade?

   A. censorship.

   B. emerging technologies.

   C. learning style research.

   D. state funding reductions.

56. Which of the following is NOT a description of the Florida certification for a school library media specialist?

   A. a bachelor's degree in any content area plus 30 hours of library/information science.

   B. a master's degree in educational media.

   C. a bachelor's degree in library/information science and a master's degree in any field of education.

   D. a bachelor's degree in any content area plus a master's in leadership/curriculum development.

57. In the Dewey Decimal System, all collective biographies are classified in

    A. 92.
    C. 031.

    B. BIO.
    D. 920.

58. In which bibliographic field should information concerning the format of an audio-visual material appear?

    A. Material specific details.

    B. Physical description.

    C. Notes.

    D. Standard numbers.

59. The on-line catalog to Florida state university libraries is

    A. ERIC.
    C. LUIS.

    B. FIRN.
    D. SIRS.

60. Southern Association accreditation standards for periodicals in a materials collection specify

    A. no fewer than 10 titles or one per every 25 students, whichever is greater.

    B. no fewer than 20 titles or one per every 100 students.

    C. one per every 20 students, not to exceed 100.

    D. one per every 10 students with no maximum.

61. Freedom of access of information for children includes all of the following except

    A. development of critical thinking.

    B. reflection of social growth.

    C. provision for religious differences.

    D. discrimination of different points of view.

62. The weekly information bulletin from the Florida Department of Education is called

    A. *School News.*

    B. *Happenings in Education.*

    C. *The Monday Report.*

    D. *Vital Signs.*

63. A periodical index search which allows the user to pair Keywords with and, but, or or is called

    A. Boolean.
    C. wildcarding.

    B. dialoguing.
    D. truncation.

64. Which of the following is the professional organization of Florida school library media specialists?

    A. FSME.
    C. FIRN.

    B. FMQ.
    D. FAME.

65. A secondary school social studies teacher reads an article in the current month's *Smithsonian* that clarifies points in the unit of study on the day prior to the scheduled unit test. He asks the media specialist if copyright law would allow copying the entire 3100 word article for distribution to each student in his two honors American history classes. The media specialist's proper response is that

A. he can make only one copy and read it to the class.

B. he may not copy it because of the word length.

C. he may excerpt sections of it to meet the brevity test.

D. he may copy the needed multiples, allowed by the spontaneity test.

66. In most learning hierarchies, which of the following is the highest order critical thinking skill?

A. appreciation.

B. inference.

C. recall.

D. comprehension.

67. The process of surrounding a slide or transparency with a cardboard or plastic frame is called

A. mounting.   C. securing.

B. framing.   D. edging.

68. An elementary school library media specialist, after reading a story to her second graders, could expect the listeners to

A. explain the story's main idea.

B. predict an alternate ending to the story.

C. recall in order the main events in the plot.

D. tell where the plot's climax occurred.

69. In the production of a teacher/student made audio-visual material, which of the following is NOT a factor in the planning phase?

A. stating the objectives.

B. analyzing the audience.

C. determining the purpose.

D. selecting the format.

70. A kindergarten class has just viewed a sound filmstrip on alligators. The best way to evaluate the suitability of the material for this age group is to

A. test the students' ability to recall the main points of the filmstrip.

B. compare this product to other similar products on this content.

C. observe the body language and verbal comments during the viewing.

D. ask the children to comment on the quality of the filmstrip at the end of the viewing.

71. **Florida certifies school library media specialists**

    A. PK-12.

    B. K-12.

    C. elementary (K-6) or secondary (7-12).

    D. elementary (K-4), middle school (5-8), or secondary (9-12).

72. **According to AASL/AECT guidelines, in her role as *instructional consultant,* the school library media specialist uses her expertise to**

    A. assist teachers in acquiring information skills which they can incorporate into classroom instruction.

    B. provide access to resource sharing systems.

    C. plan lessons in media production.

    D. provide staff development activities in equipment use.

73. **The responsibility for appointing a reconsideration committee to examine a challenged material belongs to**

    A. the school superintendent.

    B. the district media supervisor.

    C. the school principal.

    D. the school library media specialist.

74. **The simplest method of editing a videotape is**

    A. pause-edit method.

    B. manual backspace method.

    C. automatic backspace method.

    D. insert edit.

75. **Television Production classes taught in Florida schools are**

    A. language arts electives.

    B. practical and fine arts electives.

    C. vocational electives.

    D. non-designated electives.

76. **The introduction to *Information Skills for Florida Schools K-12* recommends flexible scheduling for**

    A. elementary school library media centers.

    B. middle school library media centers.

    C. secondary school library media centers.

    D. all school library media centers.

77. **Which of the following is NOT an expert in child development?**

    A. Lawrence Kohlberg.

    B. James Naisbitt.

    C. Jean Piaget.

    D. Erik Erikson.

78. A student looks for a specific title on domestic violence. When he learns it is overdue, he asks the library media specialist to tell him the borrower's name. The library media specialist should first

    A. readily reveal the borrower's name.

    B. suggest he look for the book in another library.

    C. offer to put the boy's name on reserve pending the book's return.

    D. offer to request an interlibrary loan.

79. A school faculty consists of a majority of teachers who resist learning to use new technologies. What can the school library media specialist do to involve them?

    A. ask the principal to sanction mandatory training sessions.

    B. promote new technology use with the distribution of easy written guides to each of the technologies in the school.

    C. work with cooperative teachers and let them try to convince their colleagues.

    D. invite them to visit the media center when other teachers and students are using technologies successfully.

80. Which writer composes young adult literature in the fantasy genre?

    A. Stephen King.

    B. Piers Anthony.

    C. Virginia Hamilton.

    D. Phyllis Whitney.

81. A high school science teacher is about to begin a frog dissection unit. Three students refuse to participate. When asked for assistance, the library media specialist should

    A. work with the teacher to design a replacement unit with print and non-print material on frog anatomy.

    B. offer to allow the student to use the library as a study hall during their class time.

    C. recommend that the student be sent to another class studying frogs without dissecting.

    D. abstain from condoning the student's refusal to work.

82. In a school that teaches television production or does a significant amount of studio videotaping, AASL/AECT guides recommend what size for the studio?

    A. 1200 sq. ft.   C. 1600 sq. ft.

    B. 1500 sq. ft.   D. 2000 sq. ft.

83. As much as possible, information skills should be taught as

    A. lessons independent of content studies.

    B. lessons to supplement content studies.

    C. lessons integrated into content studies.

    D. lessons enriched by content studies.

84. If the library media specialist in an accredited middle school of 1000 students had an inventory of 8800 books, to replace those missing 1200 titles, what percentage of the budget should be used?

A. 3%-5%   C. 10%-15%

B. 5%-10%   D. 20%-25%

85. An accredited elementary school has maintained an acceptable number of items in its print collection for ten years. In the evaluation review, this fact is evidence of both

A. diagnostic and projective standards.

B. diagnostic and quantitative standards.

C. projective and quantitative standards.

D. projective and qualitative standards.

86. Which of the following is an appropriately worded objective for the goal: To provide materials and services to enhance the School-to-Work Program?

A. to purchase career books equal to 5% of the total collection.

B. to increase the career book collection by 50% in the next three years.

C. to add materials on careers as funds become available.

D. to secure grant for career book purchase.

87. The principal is completing the annual report. He needs to include substantive data on use of the media center. In addition to the number of book circulations, he would like to know the proportionate use of the media center's facilities and services by the various grade levels or content areas. This information can most quickly obtained from

A. the class scheduling log.

B. student surveys.

C. lesson plans.

D. inventory figures.

88. Which member of the school library media advisory committee should contribute information primarily related to identifying materials and activities to fulfill specific learning needs?

A. principal   C. media specialist

B. teacher   D. student

89. Which of the following tasks should a volunteer NOT be asked to perform?

A. decorating bulletin boards.

B. demonstrating use of retrieval systems.

C. maintaining bookkeeping records.

D. fundraising.

90. Which of the following statements is true of media center operating budgets in Florida?

A. The state follows a prescribed system of categorical funding directly to districts for use in media centers.

B. Media center funds are appropriated from the district operating budget and allocated to schools at district level discretion.

C. School boards have control over budget allocations which may be made part of the total school package or may be administered on a per capita figure determined annually.

D. School principals determine the operating budget total from the school allocation.

91. Section 108 of the Copyright Act permits the copying of an entire book if three conditions are met. Which of the following is NOT one of those conditions?

A. The library intends to allow inter-library loan of the book.

B. The library is an archival library.

C. The copyright notice appears on all the copies.

D. The library is a public library.

92. Which of the following is determined first in deciding a media production format?

A. the size and style of the artwork.

B. the production equipment.

C. the production materials.

D. the method of display.

93. The most appropriate piece of equipment for enlarging small pictures for tracing to poster size on a wall is the

A. overhead projector.

B. opaque projector.

C. copy stand.

D. LCD panel.

94. Research has proven the value of school library media centers to student achievement. The single most important factor in improving that achievement is the media center's

A. services.   C. personnel.

B. materials   D. equipment.

95. Which of the following is NOT one of three general criteria for selection of all materials?

A. authenticity.

B. appeal.

C. appropriateness.

D. allocation.

96. **AASL/AECT guidelines recommend that student library aides be**

    A. rewarded with grades or certificates for their service.

    B. allowed to assist only during free time.

    C. allowed to perform para-professional duties.

    D. assigned tasks that relate to maintaining the atmosphere of the media center.

97. **Current judicial rulings on censorship issues will most likely be discussed in**

    A. *Kirkus Reviews.*

    B. *School Library Media Review.*

    C. *New Media.*

    D. *Newsletter of Intellectual Freedom.*

98. **Instruction provided via satellite or cable television is called**

    A. home study.

    B. distance learning.

    C. extension services.

    D. telecommunications.

99. **The Student Right to Read Statement was formulated by the**

    A. AECT.   C. NCTE.

    B. ALA.   D. FAME.

100. **The most efficient method of evaluating support staff is to**

    A. administer a written test.

    B. survey faculty whom they serve.

    C. observe their performance.

    D. obtain verbal confirmation during an employee interview.

101. **The first step in planning a training program for untrained support staff is**

    A. assessing the employee's existing skills.

    B. identifying and prioritizing skills from the job description/ evaluation instrument.

    C. determining the time schedule for the completion of training.

    D. studying the resume' and speak to former employers.

102. **Which of the following resources delineates eleven levels of involvement of the school library media center?**

    A. *Administering the School Library Media Center.*

    B. *Information Power.*

    C. *Taxonomies of the School Library Media Center.*

    D. *School Library Media Annual.*

103. In the landmark U.S. Supreme Court ruling in favor of Pico, the court's opinion established that

   A. library books, being optional not required reading, could not be arbitrarily removed by school boards.

   B. school boards have the same jurisdiction over library books as they have over textbooks.

   C. the intent to remove pervasively vulgar material is the same as the intent to deny free access to ideas.

   D. First Amendment challenges in regards to library books are the responsibility of appeals courts.

104. Preview and evaluation of commercial media products is the responsibility of

   A. district media personnel.

   B. school library media specialists and teachers.

   C. teachers and students.

   D. media specialists, teachers, and students.

105. When determining a specific piece of equipment to purchase, the school library media specialist should first consult

   A. local vendors for a demonstration.

   B. reviews in technology periodicals.

   C. manufacturers' catalogs for specifications.

   D. the state bid list for price.

106. An elementary teacher, planning a unit on the local environment, finds materials that are too global or above her students' ability level. The beset solution to this problem is to

   A. broaden the scope of the study to emphasize global concerns.

   B. eliminate the unit from the content.

   C. replace the unit with another unit that teaches the same skills.

   D. have the students design their own study materials using media production techniques.

107. Staff development activities in the use of materials and equipment are most effective if they

   A. are conducted individually as need is expressed.

   B. are sequenced in difficulty of operation or use.

   C. result in use of the acquired skills in classroom lessons.

   D. are evaluated for effectiveness.

108. A request from a social studies for the creation of a list of historical fiction titles for a book report assignment is a _____ request.

   A. ready reference.

   B. research.

   C. specific needs.

   D. complex search.

109. In formulating an estimated collection budget consider all of the following except

   A. attrition by loss, damage, or age.

   B. the maximum cost of item replacement.

   C. the number of students served.

   D. the need for expansion to meet minimum guidelines.

110. The greatest benefit of learning media production techniques is that it helps

   A. the school reduce the need to purchase commercial products.

   B. the producer clarify his learning objectives.

   C. the teacher individualize instruction.

   D. the school library media specialist integrate information skills.

111. Which of the following are projective evaluation criteria?

   A. national guidelines recommended by AASL/AECT.

   B. the commendations and recommendations of a regional accreditation committee.

   C. a school inventory of materials and equipment.

   D. personnel evaluations.

112. Recertification requirements for Florida school library media specialists mandates completion of equivalent to

   A. 6 hours of college credit every 5 years.

   B 6 hours of college credit every 10 years.

   C. 9 hours of college credit every 5 years.

   D. 12 hours of college credit every 10 years.

113. A fourth grader using *World Book Encyclopedia* cannot find an article on bullfinches in the B volume. The best solution to her problem is to

   A. tell her to look in another encyclopedia.

   B. show her how to use the index in the last volume of *World Book*.

   C. direct her to the automated card catalog.

   D. find the article for her.

114. Collection development policies are developed to accomplish all of the following except

   A. guarantee users freedom to access information.

   B. recognize the needs and interests of users.

   C. coordinate selection criteria and budget concerns.

   D. recognize rights of individuals or groups to challenge these policies.

115. **Who followed Shirley Aaron and Pat Scales as managing editor of** *School Library Media Annual?*

    A. Jane Smith.

    B. Phyllis Van Orden.

    C. David Loertscher.

    D. Emanuel Prostano.

116. **Which of the school library media specialist's roles is least recognized by school principals?**

    A. instructional consultant.

    B. staff development consultant.

    C. information specialist.

    D. curriculum planner.

117. **According to research on promotion techniques and support for library media programs, their staunchest ally must be the**

    A. teaching faculty.

    B. student body.

    C. district media supervisor.

    D. school principal.

118. **After reading** *The Pearl,* **a tenth grader asks, "Why can't we start sentences with** *and* **like John Steinbeck?" This student is showing the ability to**

    A. appreciate.   C. infer.

    B. comprehend.   D. evaluate.

119. **Which of the following is the most efficient method of assessing learner needs prior to designing information skills instruction?**

    A. consulting with media specialists in feeder schools.

    B. surveying segments of the student body.

    C. administering a written pretest.

    D. conducting informal interviews with selected students.

120. **In assessing learning styles for staff development, consider that adults**

    A. are less affected by learning environment than children.

    B. are more receptive to performing in and in front of groups.

    C. learn better when external motivations are guaranteed.

    D. demand little feedback.

121. **As a member of the school's curriculum team, the library media specialist's role would include all of the following except**

    A. ensuring a systematic approach to integrating information skills instruction.

    B. advising staff on appropriate learning styles to meet specific objectives.

    C. advising staff of current trends in curriculum design.

    D. advising staff of objectives design for specific content areas.

122. The learning trend affecting library media centers most in the 1990's is

    A. team teaching.

    B. mainstreaming.

    C. cooperative learning.

    D. multiple intelligences.

123. Which of the following is the most desirable learning outcome of a staff development workshop on *Teaching with Videodisks*? Participants

    A. score 80% or better on a post-test.

    B. design content specific lessons from multiple resources.

    C. sign up to take additional workshops.

    D. encourage other teachers to participate in future workshops.

124. According to current research, the biggest concern in media education in Florida is the crisis of

    A. the lack of qualified personnel.

    B. failure to keep abreast of technology advances.

    C. the failure of legislation to address library media needs.

    D. widespread illiteracy.

125. The director of the Division of School Media Services for the Florida Department of Education is responsible for

    A. participation on curriculum development teams.

    B. development of guidelines for the accreditation of schools.

    C. seeking legislative initiatives and support for library media programs.

    D. seeking grants from federal sources for the improvement of school media centers.

ANSWER KEY

#		#		#		#		#		#	
1.	D	23.	C	45.	B	67.	A	89.	C	111.	A
2.	B	24.	B	46.	B	68.	C	90.	C	112.	A
3.	B	25.	D	47.	C	69.	D	91.	A	113.	B
4.	B	26.	C	48.	C	70.	C	92.	D	114.	C
5.	A	27.	C	49.	B	71.	B	93.	B	115.	A
6.	B	28.	A	50.	B	72.	D	94.	C	116.	D
7.	C	29.	C	51.	A	73.	B	95.	D	117.	D
8.	B	30.	D	52.	D	74.	A	96.	A	118.	D
9.	B	31.	B	53.	A	75.	C	97.	D	119.	C
10.	A	32.	A	54.	C	76.	D	98.	B	120.	B
11.	B	33.	C	55.	B	77.	B	99.	C	121.	D
12.	B	34.	A	56.	D	78.	C	100.	C	122.	C
13.	C	35.	D	57.	D	79.	D	101.	B	123.	B
14.	A	36.	B	58.	C	80.	B	102.	C	124.	A
15.	B	37.	D	59.	C	81.	A	103.	A	125.	C
16.	D	38.	B	60.	A	82.	C	104.	D		
17.	B	39.	B	61.	C	83.	C	105.	C		
18.	A	40.	C	62.	C	84.	C	106.	D		
19.	B	41.	B	63.	A	85.	B	107.	C		
20.	C	42.	D	64.	D	86.	B	108.	C		
21.	B	43.	C	65.	D	87.	A	109.	B		
22.	C	44.	C	66.	B	88.	D	110.	B		

"Mrs. Hammond, I'd know you anywhere from little Billy's portrait of you."

"Are we there yet?"

"Gosh, now we've seen everything!"

700436

Printed in the United States
28062LVS00002B/187-188